# ARISTOTLE'S POETICS

# ARISTOTLE'S
## *POETICS*

*Translated by S. H. Butcher*

*Introduction by*

## FRANCIS FERGUSSON

 HILL AND WANG · NEW YORK

Hill and Wang
A division of Farrar, Straus and Giroux
19 Union Square West, New York 10003

Introduction copyright © 1961 by Francis Fergusson
All rights reserved
Distributed in Canada by Douglas & McIntyre Ltd.
Printed in the United States of America
First edition, 1961

Library of Congress Catalog Card Number: 61-6943
Paperback ISBN: 0-8090-0527-1

The translation of *The Poetics* is reprinted by
permission of Macmillan & Company Ltd. and the
Executors of the Estate of S. H. Butcher.

www.fsgbooks.com

55   57   58   56

# CONTENTS

# INTRODUCTION

# I. THE *POETICS*
## AND THE MODERN READER

The *Poetics*, short as it is, is the most fundamental study we have of the art of drama. It has been used again and again, since the text was recovered in the early Renaissance, as a guide to the techniques of play-making, and as the basis of various theories of drama. In our own time the great Marxist playwright, Bertolt Brecht, started with it in working out his own methods. He thought that all drama before him was constructed on Aristotle's principles, and that his own "epic drama" was the first strictly non-Aristotelian form.

When Aristotle wrote the *Poetics*, in the fourth century B.C., he had the Greek theater before his eyes, the first theater in our tradition. Perhaps that is why he could go straight to the basis of the dramatic art: he "got in on the ground floor." There is a majestic simplicity about the opening sentence, which we (in our more complex world) can only envy: "I propose to treat of Poetry in itself and of its various kinds, noting the essential quality of each. . . ." It still appears that, for tragedy at least, his favorite form, he did just that.

But the *Poetics* is not so simple for us as that sentence suggests. In the two thousand years of its life it has been lost, found again, and fought over by learned interpreters in every period. The modern reader, approaching it for the first time, may benefit from a little assistance.

The text itself is incomplete, repetitious in spots, and badly organized. It probably represents part of a set of lecture notes, with later interpolations. Our text is the translation of the late S. H. Butcher, who also edited the Greek from the sources. It is one of the standard texts, probably the best now available in English. The reader will find Butcher's "Analytical Table of Contents" on pages 45-48 a useful guide on a first reading. Each chapter is summarized, and the main interpolations and omissions are indicated.

In writing the *Poetics* Aristotle apparently assumed that his readers would know his own philosophy, and also the plays and poems he discusses. Certain key terms, like "action," "pathos," "form," can only be fully understood in the light of Aristotle's other writings. Moreover, his whole method is empirical: he starts with works of art that he knew well, and tries to see in them what the poet was aiming at, and how he put his play or poem together. He does not intend the *Poetics* to be an exact science, or even a textbook with strict laws, as the Renaissance humanists tried to make out with their famous "rules" of the unities of time, place, and action. He knew that every poet has his unique vision, and must therefore use the principles of his art in his own way. The *Poetics* is much more like a cookbook than it is like a textbook in elementary engineering.

The *Poetics* should therefore be read slowly, as an "aid to reflection"; only then does Aristotle's coherent conception of the art of drama emerge. In what follows I shall offer a short reading of this kind: bringing out the main course of his thought; pausing to see what he means by his notions of human psychology and conduct; and illustrating his artistic principles by actual plays. For the sake of convenience I shall use Sophocles' *Oedipus Rex*,

Aristotle's own favorite tragedy, as my main illustration. But of course the art of drama is the matter in hand, and the more plays one analyzes in the light of Aristotle's principles, the better one understands the scope and value of the *Poetics*.

## II. PRELIMINARY OBSERVATIONS ON POETRY AND OTHER ARTS (CHAPTERS I–V)

The opening chapters of the *Poetics* appear to be an introduction to a longer work (which has not survived) on the major forms of Poetry known to Aristotle, including comedy, epic, and dithyrambic poetry, as well as tragedy. The *Poetics* as it has come down to us, however, is devoted mainly to tragedy, and it is in Aristotle's analysis of that form that his general theory of art is most clearly illustrated. The first five chapters should be read, therefore, as a preliminary sketch which Aristotle will fill in when he gets down to business in Chapter VI.

Poets, like painters, musicians, and dancers, Aristotle says, all "imitate action" in their various ways. By "action" he means, not physical activity, but a movement-of-spirit, and by "imitation" he means, not superficial copying, but the representation of the countless forms which the life of the human spirit may take, in the media of the arts: musical sound, paint, word, or gesture. Aristotle does not discuss this idea here, for it was a commonplace, in his time, that the arts all (in some sense) imitate action.

The arts may be distinguished in three ways: according to the *object* imitated, the *medium* em-

ployed, and the manner. The object is always a
particular action. The writer of tragedy (as we
shall see) imitates a "serious and complete action";
the writer of comedy, one performed by characters
who are "worse"—by which Aristotle may mean
"sillier"—than the people we know in real life. By
"medium" he simply means the poet's words, or the
painter's colors, or the musician's sound. By "manner" he means something like "convention." Thus
the manner of the writer of epics (or novels) is to
represent the action in his own words; that of the
playwright to represent it by what characters, acted
on a stage, do and say. One may use the notions
of object, medium, and manner still, to give a rough
classification of the varied forms of poetry we know
in our day.

In Chapter IV Aristotle briefly raises the question of the origin and development of poetry,
which includes all the forms of literature and drama.
He thinks it comes from two instincts in human
nature itself, that of imitation and that of harmony
and rhythm. The pleasure we get from the imitations of art is quite different from direct experience: it seems to come from recognizing what
the artist is representing; some experience or vague
intuition which suddenly seems familiar. It satisfies
our need to know and understand; imitation has
to do with the intellectual and moral content of art,
and is therefore related to philosophy. Harmony
and rhythm, on the other hand, refers to the
pleasures of form which we usually consider
"purely esthetic." It is characteristic of Aristotle to
recognize both the content and the form of art.

After this short but suggestive passage, Aristotle
sketches the historic development of the dithyramb,

comedy, epic, and tragedy, in Greece. The passage is important, for it is the starting point of modern investigations of the sources of literature and the theater in our tradition, but Aristotle has, at this point, very little to say. It has been left to modern anthropologists and historians to fill in the details as well as they could, and I shall have something to say of their theories on pages 36 to 40.

Aristotle did not have our interest in history, nor did he believe, as we often do, that the most primitive forms of human culture were the most significant. He thought that the only way to understand man, or his institutions, or his arts, was in their most fully developed, or "perfected" state. In the *Poetics* he seeks the highest forms of the art, and the masterpieces within each form, in order to see, in them, what poetry may be; and so he is led to tragedy. "Whether Tragedy has as yet perfected its proper types or not . . . raises another question," he writes (IV.11); but tragedy was the form known to him which best fulfilled the aims of poetry, and most fully employed the resources of that art. He leaves room (in his usual cautious way) for the possible appearance of other forms; meanwhile he takes Greek tragedy, and especially Sophocles' masterpiece, *Oedipus Rex*, as his main instance of what poetry can be.

In Chapter V Aristotle begins a discussion of comedy, but this part is fragmentary, and not enough survives to tell us what he thought of that art. In Chapters XXIII and XXVI he discusses epic, but he thinks the principles of epic are only corollaries of those of tragedy, the more complete form. It is his analysis of tragedy, which begins in Chapter

VI, that constitutes the main argument in the *Poetics*.

## III. TRAGEDY: AN IMITATION OF AN ACTION

In Chapter VI.2, Aristotle starts his analysis of the art of tragedy with his famous definition:

Tragedy, then, is an imitation of an action that is serious, complete, and of a certain magnitude; in language embellished with each kind of artistic ornament, the several kinds being found in separate parts of the play; in the form of action, not of narrative; through pity and fear effecting the proper purgation of these emotions.

This definition is intended to describe tragedy, and also to distinguish it from other forms of poetry. Greek tragedy employed a verse form near to prose, like our English blank verse, for the dialogue, and elaborate lyric forms with musical accompaniment for the choruses; that is what Aristotle means by the different kinds of language. It is "in the form of action"—that is, it is acted on a stage—unlike epic, which is merely told by one voice. The "purgation of pity and fear" is Aristotle's description of the special *kind* of pleasure we get from tragedy.

The play itself, as we read it or see it performed, is the "imitation" of an action, and in what follows Aristotle devotes his attention, not to the action, but to the making of the play which represents an action. He is concerned with the *art* of tragedy; the phases of the poet's work of play-making. The six "parts of Tragedy" which he discusses are, in

fact, part of the poet's creative labor, and should
be translated, "plot-*making*," "character *delineation*," and so forth. But before one can understand
Aristotle's account of the poet's *art*, one must know
what the art is trying to represent: the vision, or
inspiration, which moves the poet to write or sing,
i.e., the "action."

## THE CONCEPT OF "ACTION"; ACTION AND PASSION

Just after the definition of tragedy (VI.5) Aristotle tells us that action springs from two "natural
causes," character and thought. A man's character disposes him to act in certain ways, but he
*actually* acts only in response to the changing circumstances of his life, and it is his thought (or
perception) that shows him what to seek and what
to avoid in each situation. Thought and character
together *make* his actions. This may serve to in-
dicate the basic meaning of "action," but if one is
to understand how the arts imitate action, one must
explore the notion a little further.

One must be clear, first of all, that *action (praxis)*
does not mean deeds, events, or physical activity:
it means, rather, the motivation from which deeds
spring. Butcher* puts it this way: "The *praxis* that
art seeks to reproduce is mainly a psychic energy
working outwards." It may be described metaphorically as the focus or movement of the psyche
toward what seems good to it at the moment—a
"movement-of-spirit," Dante calls it. When we try
to define the actions of people we know, or of
characters in plays, we usually do so in terms of

* *Aristotle's Theory of Poetry and Fine Art*, by S. H.
Butcher. 4th ed., London: 1932.

motive. In the beginning of *Oedipus Rex*, for instance, Oedipus learns that the plague in Thebes is due to the anger of the gods, who are offended because the murderer of old King Laius was never found and punished. At that point Oedipus's action arises, i.e., his motive is formed: "to find the slayer." His action so defined continues, with many variations in response to changing situations, until he finds the slayer, who of course turns out to be himself. When Aristotle says "action" (*praxis*) in the *Poetics*, he usually means the whole working out of a motive to its end in success or failure.

Oedipus's action in most of the play is easy to define; his motive is a clear and rational purpose. That is the kind of action which Aristotle usually has in mind in discussing tragedy, and his word *praxis* connotes rational purpose. The common motive "to find the slayer" accounts for the main movement of *Oedipus Rex;* and most drama, which must be instantly intelligible to an audience, depends on such clearly defined motivation. But we know that human motivation is of many kinds, and in *Oedipus Rex*, or any great play, we can see that the characters are also moved by feelings they hardly understand, or respond to ideas or visions which are illusory. When one thinks of the other arts that imitate action, it is even more obvious that "rational purpose" will not cover all action: what kind of "movement-of-spirit" is represented in music, or painting, or lyric verse? "The unity of action," Coleridge wrote,* "is not properly a rule, but in itself the great end, not only of drama, but of the lyric, epic, even to the candle-flame of the epigram—not only of poetry, but of poesy in

* In his essay on *Othello*.

general, as the proper generic term inclusive of all the fine arts as its species." That is exactly Aristotle's view. He sees an action represented in every work of art, and the arts reflect not only rational purpose but movements-of-spirit of every kind.

In the *Poetics* Aristotle assumes, but does not explain, his more general concept of action. Thus when he writes (VI.9), "life consists in action, and its end is a mode of action," he is referring to the concept as explained in his writings on ethics. The word he uses there to cover any movement-of-spirit is *energeia*. In his studies of human conduct he speaks of three different forms of *energeia*, which he calls *praxis*, *poiesis*, and *theoria*. In *praxis* the motive is "to do" something; we have seen that Oedipus's action, as soon as he sees that he must find the slayer, is a *praxis*. In *poiesis* the motive is "to make" something; it is the action of artists when they are focused upon the play, or the song, or the poem, which they are trying to *make*. Our word "poetry" comes from this Greek word, and the *Poetics* itself is an analysis of the poet's action in making a tragedy. In *theoria* the motive is "to grasp and understand" some truth. It may be translated as "contemplation," if one remembers that, for Aristotle, contemplation is intensely active. When he says (VI.9) that the end of life is a mode of action, he means *theoria*. He thought that "all men wish to know," and that the human spirit lives most fully and intensely in the perception of truth.

These three modes of action—doing, making, and contemplation—provide only a very rough classification of human actions, and Aristotle is well aware of that. For every action arises in a particular character, in response to the particular situation he perceives at that moment: every action has its own form or mode of being. Moreover, in Aristotle's psychology, both action and character (which he defines as *habitual action*) are formed out of ill-defined feelings and emotions, which he calls *pathos*. In any tragedy, which must represent a "complete action," the element of pathos is essential. If we are to understand the action in our example, *Oedipus Rex*, we must reflect upon the relationship between the pathos with which the play begins and ends, and the common purpose, to find the slayer, that produces the events of the story.

In Aristotle's philosophy, and in many subsequent theories of human conduct, the concepts "action" and "passion" (or *praxis* and *pathos*), are sharply contrasted. Action is active: the psyche perceives something it wants, and "moves" toward it. Passion is passive: the psyche suffers something it cannot control or understand, and "is moved" thereby. The two concepts, abstractly considered, are opposites; but in our human experience action and passion are always combined, and that fact is recognized in Aristotle's psychology. There is no movement of the psyche which is pure passion—totally devoid of purpose and understanding—except perhaps in some pathological states where the human quality is lost. And there is no human action without its component of ill-defined feeling or emotion; only God (in some Aristotelian philosophies) may be defined as Pure Act. When Aristotle says "life consists in action," he is thinking of action, in its countless forms, continually arising out of the more formless pathos (or "affectivity," as we call it) of the human psyche. Even in pain, lust, terror, or grief, the passion, as we know it, acquires some more or less conscious motive, some recognizably human form. That is why Aristotle can speak (XVIII.2) both of "pathetic" motivation, which is closer to the passionate pole of experience, and "ethical" motivation, which is closer to reason and the consciously controlled will.

With these considerations in mind, one can see more clearly what Aristotle means by the "complete action" which a tragedy represents. In the Prologue of *Oedipus Rex*, Thebes is suffering under the plague, and the Citizens beseech King Oedipus for help: the common purpose, "to cure Thebes," arises out of the passion of fear. When Creon brings the Oracle's word, the action is more sharply defined as "to find the slayer." Each Episode is a dispute between Oedipus and one of his antagonists about the quest for the slayer, and each one ends as the disputants fail to agree, and new facts are brought to light. The Chorus is left a prey to its fear again. The Choral Odes are "pathetic" in motivation, but their pathos, or passion, is given form through the continued effort *to see* how the common purpose might still be achieved. When Oedipus at last finds himself to be the culprit, his action is shattered, and even his character as an ethically responsible man along with it. The Chorus suffers with him; but through the laments and terrible visions of the end of the play, their action moves to *its* end: they see the culprit, and thereby the salvation of the city. Moreover, they see in self-blinded Oedipus a general truth of the human condition:

Men of Thebes: look upon Oedipus.

This is the king who solved the famous riddle
And towered up, most powerful of men.

> No mortal eyes but looked on him with envy.
> Yet in the end ruin swept over him.
>
> Let every man in mankind's frailty
> Consider his last day; and let none
> Presume on his good fortune until he find
> Life, at his death, a memory without pain.*

This marks the end of the action in more ways than one. The common purpose has reached its paradoxical success, and the Chorus (and through it, the audience) has attained that mode of action, *theoria*, contemplation of the truth, which Aristotle regarded as the ultimate goal of a truly human life. The complete action represented in *Oedipus Rex* is (fortunately for our purposes) easy to see. But all human actions which are worked out to the end, passing through the unforeseeable contingencies of a "world we never made," follow a similar course: the conscious purpose with which they start is redefined after each unforeseen contingency is suffered; and at the end, in the light of hindsight, we see the truth of what we have been doing. Mr. Kenneth Burke has used this "tragic rhythm of action," as he calls it, Purpose, to Passion, to Perception, in his illuminating analyses of various kinds of literature. All serious works of fiction or drama represent some complete action, even so complex a form as Shakespearean tragedy. In short, Aristotle's notion is useful still; for his lore of "action" is a kind of natural history of the psyche's life.

### HOW PLOT-MAKING IMITATES THE ACTION

Plot-making is in bad odor with contemporary critics of poetry, because they think of it as the

---

* *Sophocles' Oedipus Rex.* An English Version by Dudley Fitts and Robert Fitzgerald. New York: 1949.

mechanical ingenuity of whodunits and other "plotty" entertainments. Aristotle saw the usefulness of that kind of plot-making, and offers suggestions about how to do it; but his own primary conception of plot is "organic." He sees the plot as the basic *form* of the play, and in that sense one might speak of the "plot" of a short lyric.

But he is discussing the making of the plot of tragedy, and his first definition of it (VI.6) applies only to drama: "the arrangement of the incidents." This definition is very useful, as a beginning, because it enables one to distinguish the plot both from the story the poet wishes to dramatize, and from the action he wishes to represent.

The *story* of Oedipus was known to Sophocles as a mass of legendary material covering several generations. In making his *plot*, he selected only a few incidents to present onstage, and represented the rest through the testimony of Tiresias, Jocasta, the Messenger from Corinth, and the old Shepherd. The distinction between plot and story applies to all plays, including those whose story is invented by the poet. The story of an Ibsen play, for instance, might be told as a three-decker novel, but Ibsen always "arranges the incidents" in such a way as to show only a few crucial moments directly.

The purpose of plot-making is to represent one "complete action," in the case of *Oedipus Rex* the quest for the slayer which I have described. We must suppose that Sophocles saw a quest, a seeking motive, in the sprawling incidents of the Oedipus legend. That would be his poetic vision or "inspiration," the first clue to the play-to-be. He saw this action as tragic: as eventuating in destruction, suffering, and the appearance of a new insight. At that moment plot-making begins; the incidents of the story begin to fall into a significant arrangement.

"Plot, then," says Aristotle (VI.15), "is the first principle, and, as it were, the soul of a tragedy." This is the organic metaphor which is so useful in the analysis of a work of art. By "soul" Aristotle (who was a biologist) means the formative principle in any live thing whether man, animal, or plant. Consider an egg, for instance: it is only potentially a chicken until the "soul" within it, through the successive phases of embryonic development, makes it *actually* a chicken. Similarly, the action which the poet first glimpses is only potentially a tragedy, until his plot-making forms it into an *actual* tragedy. Aristotle thought that when the incidents of the story are arranged in their tragic sequence, they already produce some of the tragic effect, even though the characters are hardly more than names. That stage would correspond to the embryo when it is first recognizable as a chicken. But the chicken is not fully actual until it has plumage and a squawk, and the tragedy is not fully actual until all the dramatis personae are characterized, and all the language is formed to express their changing actions, moment by moment. The plot, in other words, is the "first" or basic form of the play, but it is by character delineation and the arts of language that the poet gives it the final form which we read, or see and hear.

## The Parts of the Plot

A complete action (as we have seen) passes through the modes of purpose and pathos to the final perception, and the plot therefore has "parts"

—types of incidents in the beginning, middle, and end of the play—resulting from the various modes of action. Aristotle discusses the parts of the plot in several ways, in connection with various play-writing problems.

In Chapter XII he lists and defines the "quantitative parts" of a tragedy, by which he means the sections (rather like the movements of a symphony) in which Greek tragedies were traditionally written: Prologue, Episode, Exode, and Choric song. This chapter is probably a late interpolation, and defective; but in the light of modern studies of the relation between tragedy and the ritual forms from which it was derived, it is important. The table on page 41 shows the "quantitative parts" of *Oedipus Rex* in relation to the action, and to the supposed form of the Dionysian ritual.

Aristotle devotes most of his attention to the "organic parts" of the plot, by which he apparently means those which represent a tragic action, and best serve to produce the specifically tragic effect. They all represent the action at the moment when it is reaching its catastrophic end: Reversal of the Situation, Recognition, and Pathos, which Butcher translates "Scene of Suffering." In the best tragedies, reversal, recognition, and pathos are inherent in the basic conception of the plot, and depend upon one another, as in *Oedipus Rex*.

"Reversal of the Situation," Aristotle says (XI.1), "is a change by which the action veers round to its opposite. . . . Thus in the *Oedipus*, the Messenger comes to cheer Oedipus and free him from his alarms about his mother, but by revealing who he is, he produces the opposite effect." Notice that the objective situation does not change, for Oedipus

was, in fact, Jocasta's son all along. What changes is
the situation as the thought of the characters makes
it out at that moment; that is why Oedipus's action
changes before our eyes. The action which seemed
to be about to reach a happy end is seen to be
headed for catastrophe, and Oedipus's final pathos
follows.

"Recognition," Aristotle writes (XI.2), ". . . is
a change from ignorance to knowledge." Oedipus's
change from ignorance to knowledge occurs as he
cross-questions the Messenger, and then the old
Shepherd. By plotting this crucial moment in this
way, Sophocles has, as it were, spread out before
our eyes the whole turn of Oedipus's inner being,
from the triumph which seems just ahead to utter
despair. The tremendous excitement of this passage
is partly due to the fact that what Oedipus "recognizes" is the reversal: "The best form of recognition is coincident with a Reversal of the Situation,
as in the *Oedipus*," says Aristotle (XI.2). And it is
due also to the fact that this moment of enlighten-
ment was inherent in the whole conception of the
Tragic Plot: ". . . of all recognitions," says Aristotle (XVI.8), "the best is that which arises from
the incidents themselves, where the startling discovery is made by natural means. Such is that in
the *Oedipus* of Sophocles."

Aristotle offers the recognition scenes in *Oedipus*
and in Sophocles' *Electra* (where the situation onstage turns from despair to triumph) as models of
their kind. He also briefly analyzes other more
mechanical and superficial ways of plotting the
passage from ignorance to knowledge. He is certainly right in calling the recognition scene an
"organic part" of the tragic plot, for in good drama

down to our own day such scenes are essential to
the tragic effect. Consider old Lear's gradual recognition of Cordelia, as he wakes in Act V; or Mrs.
Alving's recognition of her son's mortal illness at
the end of *Ghosts*. The action of perceiving, passing
from ignorance to knowledge, is near the heart of
tragedy, and the masters of that art all know how
to "arrange the incidents" in such a way as to
represent it on the stage.

Pathos also is an essential element in tragedy. We
have seen that the whole action of *Oedipus Rex*
arises out of the passion of fear; sinks back into
pathos in each of the Choral Odes, and ends in the
long sequence when the Chorus finally sees the
meaning of Oedipus's suffering. Aristotle has little
to say about plotting the "scene of suffering," perhaps because in Greek tragedy the element of pathos
is usually represented in the musically accompanied
verse of the Choral Odes. His most important point
is in Chapter XIV.1: "Fear and Pity may be aroused
by spectacular means; but they may also result
from the inner structure of the piece. . . . He who
hears the tale told will thrill with horror and melt
to pity at what takes place. This is the impression
we should receive from hearing the story of the
*Oedipus*." When Oedipus yells in agony, when he
appears with bleeding sockets for eyes, pathos is
certainly represented by "spectacular means"; but
by that moment in the play we understand Oedipus's plight so deeply that the sights and sounds
are only symbols of the destruction of his inner
being.

In discussing the "organic parts of the Plot" Aristotle has nothing to say about the Episodes. In
*Oedipus Rex* the Episodes are the fierce disputes

between Oedipus and his antagonists, whereby the quest for the slayer moves to its unforeseen end; they are essential in the unfolding of the story. Perhaps the text is again defective here, or it may be that Aristotle thought the Episodes less essential to the tragic effect than reversal, recognition, and pathos. However that may be, the inner structure of the Episodes, which are public debates, struggles of mind against mind, may best be considered under the heading of Thought and Diction, and I shall have something to say of them on page 26.

## Kinds of Plots

Since the vision which the poet is trying to represent in his play is a certain action, there are various kinds of plot-making appropriate to the various kinds of action. The *Oedipus* is (in Aristotle's view) the best model: the action is "complete" and the plot represents it almost perfectly. The plot is "Complex," by which Aristotle means that it includes reversal and recognition, but there are "Simple Plots" which do not include these elements. The plot of *The Death of a Salesman*, for example, is simple, for poor Willy Loman proceeds straight down to his sordid end without ever passing from ignorance to knowledge. The action of *Oedipus Rex* takes the form of "ethical" motivation as Oedipus pursues his rational and morally responsible purpose of finding the slayer, as well as "pathetic" motivation at the beginning and end of the play. But Aristotle also recognizes plays of essentially pathetic motivation, and plays of essentially ethical motivation. In our time, Chekhov's plays are pathetic in motivation, and the plot, or basic form, is more like that of a lyric than that of traditional "drama." Ibsen's plays are mainly ethical in motivation, and consist chiefly of disputes like the Episodes in *Oedipus*.

Aristotle never forgets that a play must, by definition, hold and please an audience in the theater, and his whole discussion of plot-making is interspersed with practical suggestions for the playwright. The story must seem "probable," and Aristotle has canny recipes for making it seem so. The supernatural is hard to put over, and it is wiser to keep the gods off the stage. In Chapter XVIII.1, Aristotle points out that any plot may be divided into two main parts, the Complication, which extends from the prologue to the turning point, and the Unraveling or denouement, from the turning point to the end. This way of describing the structure of a plot will sound familiar to anyone who has learned the mechanics of the "well-made play." It is a useful formula for the practical playwright, because it has to do, not with the dramatist's vision, but with the *means* of making any action clear and effective in the theater.

Aristotle's practical suggestions are still valuable, but they require no explanation, and I return to his main theory.

### The Unity of the Play; Double Plots

The most fundamental question one can ask about any work of art is that of its unity: how do its parts cohere in order to make *one* beautiful object? Aristotle's answer, which he emphasizes again and again, is that a play or poem can be unified only if it represents *one action*. The poet, in building his form, conceiving his characters, writing his words, must make sure that everything embodies the one movement-of-spirit. That, as Coleridge says, is a counsel of perfection, "not properly a rule," but rather what all the arts aim at.

The plot of a play is the first form of the one action; what then are we to say of plays, like many of Shakespeare's, in which several plots, often taken from different stories, are combined?

Aristotle of course did not have Shakespeare's plays, but he did have Homer, who also combined many stories, many plot sequences, both in the *Iliad* and the *Odyssey*. And he recognized that Homer unified that more complex scheme by obeying the fundamental requirement of unity of action: (VIII.3): ". . . he made the *Odyssey*, and likewise the *Iliad*, to center round an action that in our sense of the word is one." Aristotle returns to this point in Chapter XXIII, where he takes up the epic. Lesser poets, he says, have tried to unify an epic by basing it upon one character, or one great historic event, like the Trojan War. Only Homer had the vision to discover one action in the wide and diversified material of his epics. The action of the *Iliad* (as the first lines suggest) is "to deal with the anger of Achilles." The action of the *Odyssey* is "to get home again," a nostalgic motive which we feel in Odysseus's wanderings, in Telemachus's wanderings, and in Penelope's patient struggle to save her home from the suitors. The interwoven stories, each with its plot, are analogous; and in the same way the stories which Shakespeare wove together to make a *Lear* or a *Hamlet* are analogous: varied embodiments of one action.

Aristotle did not think that tragedies plotted like

the *Odyssey* with "a double thread of plot" (XIII.7) were the best tragedies. He preferred the stricter unity of the single plot and the single catastrophe. Perhaps if he had read *Lear* or *Hamlet* he would have modified this view. Even so, his principle of the unity of action is still the best way we have to describe the unity of a work of art, including the vast and complex ones with two or more plots.

## HOW CHARACTER DELINEATION IMITATES THE ACTION

In Aristotle's diagrammatic account of play-making, the poet works on characterization after the action has been plotted as a tragic sequence of incidents. Characters are of course implicit from the first, since all actions are actions of individuals. But, as Aristotle reminds us again and again, ". . . tragedy is an imitation, not of men, but of an action and of life" (VI.9), and therefore "character comes in as subsidiary to the actions." The poet sees the action of the play-to-be first; then its tragic form (or plot), and then the characters best fitted to carry it out with variety and depth.

One must remember that in Aristotle's psychology, character is less fundamental than action. *Character* is defined as "habitual action," and it is formed by parents and other environmental influences out of the comparatively formless pathos (appetites, fears, and the like) which move the very young. As the growing person acquires habitual motives, he begins to understand them rationally, and so becomes ethically responsible: we say that he is a good or bad *character*. When we first meet Oedipus, he is a fully-formed character: a re-

sponsible ruler who (apparently in full awareness
of what he is doing) adopts the rational motive of
finding the slayer of Laius. But his discovery that
he is himself the culprit destroys, not only his
motive, but the "character" of knowing and responsible ruler; and passion, or pathos, takes over.
Old Lear, at a similar point in his story, describes
the experience accurately:

> O, how this mother swells up toward my heart!
> Hysterica passio! Down, thou climbing sorrow,
> Thy element's below.

After the catastrophes both Lear and Oedipus are
"pathetically" motivated, like children, and like
children ask for help and guidance. In tragedy,
character is often destroyed; and at that moment
we can glimpse "life and action" at a deeper level.

It is easy to see how the character of Oedipus,
as imagined by Sophocles, is admirably fitted to
represent the main action of the play, and carry it
all the way to the end. With his intelligence, his
arrogant self-confidence, and his moral courage, he
is the perfect protagonist. But the other characters
are almost equally effective for this purpose: Tiresias, who knows the will of the gods all along, but
cannot himself take the lead in cleansing the city;
or Jocasta, who obscurely fears the truth, and so
feels that Thebes would be better off in ignorance.
The contrasting characters reveal the main action
in different ways, and their disagreements make the
tense disputes of all the Episodes. But all this
diversity of characterization, all this conflict of
thought, is "with a view" to the action of the play
as a whole: that common motive which I have said

is "to save Thebes from its plague, by finding the unknown culprit."

It is, of course, by the plot that this main action, or common motive, is established. It is very clear in the Prologue, when everyone wants only to save Thebes. We forget it in the excitement of the disputes, and in the fascination of the contrasted characters; but we are reminded of it again in each Choral Ode. It is the Chorus which most directly represents the action of the *play;* and the Chorus can do that just because it has less "character" than Oedipus or his antagonists. In the Chorus we can sense the action at a deeper-than-individual level, and its successive Odes, with music and dance, mark the life and movement of the *play*.

We must suppose that the actions of Tiresias, Jocasta, even Oedipus, would be quite different if we saw them apart from the basic situation of the play—the plague in Thebes. We see them only in relation to that crisis, and that is why their actions, different though their characters are, are analogous. Aristotle has a good deal to say (VI.11 and 12) about less successful kinds of character delineation. Some of our "modern poets," he says, do not make effective characters, and so their works are devoid of ethical quality. Others develop character for its own sake—for local color, perhaps, or glamour, or amusement—thereby weakening the unity of the play, which can only be achieved when the action is one. In *Oedipus Rex* this problem is beautifully solved: the characters, sharply contrasted, are full of individual life and varied "ethical quality," yet the action of the *play* underlies them all.

Aristotle offers many other ideas about character delineation, based on his observation of the theater

he knew, notably in Chapters XIII and XV. They
are essentially practical rules of thumb, intended to
assist the playwright to succeed with his audience,
like his insistence on "probability" and consistency
in characterization, or his notion that the tragic
protagonist should usually be a ruler or leader. His
observations are shrewd; but to be of assistance now
they must be translated into terms of the modern
theater.

## HOW "THOUGHT AND DICTION" IMITATE THE ACTION

In Chapter XIX Aristotle takes up "Thought"
and "Diction" together, for they are both aspects
of the language of the play. By *Diction*, he tells us,
he means "the art of delivery": diction or speech
as it is taught in modern schools of acting. Diction
is one of the six parts of tragedy, for tragedy is by
definition acted on a stage, and the actors must
know how to handle its language. But Aristotle has
little to say about it, because he is studying the
art of the poet, who does not have to know how
to speak as actors do.

Thought, however, concerns the poet directly,
for thought is one of the "causes" of action. The
poet works it out after the situations of the plot,
and the characters, are clearly conceived. The word
"thought" (*dianoia*) refers to a very wide range of
the mind's activities, from abstract reasoning to the
perception and formulation of emotion; for it is
thought that defines all the objects of human motivation, whether they are dimly seen or clear and
definite, illusory as dream, or objectively real. In
the play, thought is represented by what the char-

acters *say* about the course to be pursued, in each situation. That is why Aristotle identifies thought with the arts of language. "Under Thought," he says (XIX.2) "is included every effect which has to be produced by speech, the subdivisions being—proof and refutation; the excitation of the feelings, such as pity, fear, anger, and the like; the suggestion of importance or its opposite." At this point Aristotle refers us to his *Rhetoric*, where these modes of discourse are analyzed in detail.

In that work he writes (I.2), "Rhetoric may be defined as the faculty of observing in any given case the available means of persuasion. . . ." (Jowett's translation.) He is thinking primarily of a public speaker, a lawyer or statesman, whose action is "to persuade" his audience to adopt his opinion. He considers the various means the speaker may use to persuade his audience: his attitudes, his use of voice and gesture, his pauses—in short, such means as actors use. But his main attention is devoted to arts of language, from the most logical (proof and refutation) where the appeal is to reason, to more highly colored language intended to move the feelings. The *Rhetoric* is an analysis of the forms of "Thought and Diction" which the action of persuading may take.

This analysis may be applied directly to the Episodes in *Oedipus*, i.e., to the thought-and-language of Oedipus and his antagonists, in the successive situations of the plot. They meet to debate a great public question, that of the welfare of Thebes; and they try to persuade not only one another, but the listening Chorus, and beyond that the frightened city. They are thus situated as Aristotle's user of rhetoric is, and they resort to the same arts of language. They begin with a show of reason ("proof and refutation"); but as this fails to persuade, they resort to more emotional language, and when that too fails the dispute is broken off in dismay.

Sophocles' Athenian audience, which was accustomed to the arts of public speaking, would presumably have enjoyed the skill of Oedipus and his antagonists. In modern drama we find neither the sophisticated formality of Greek tragedy, nor the rhetorical virtuosity which Aristotle analyzes. But the principles, both of tragedy and of classical rhetoric, are natural, and disputants in our day—politicians or mere amateur arguers—resort to rhetorical forms, whether they have ever heard of them or not. Disputing characters in all drama—especially drama of "ethical" motivation like Ibsen's—instinctively use the stratagems of rhetoric, as they try to overcome each other with thought-and-language. The structure of great scenes of conflict, in Neoclassic French drama, in Shakespeare, in Ibsen, is in this respect similar to that of the Episodes in *Oedipus*.

At this point the logic of Aristotle's scheme seems to require an analysis of the language of the Choral Odes which follow each Episode. In glossing his definition of tragedy he explains (VI.3), "By 'language embellished' I mean language into which rhythm, 'harmony,' and song enter"—which must refer to the Odes with their musical accompaniment. And he emphasizes the importance of the Chorus in the structure of the play (XVIII.7): "The Chorus too should be regarded as one of the actors; it should be an integral part of the whole, and share in the action, in the manner not of

Euripides but of Sophocles." We know from his
remark on *Mousiké*, which includes both music and
lyric verse (in his *Politics*, VIII) that he thought
the modes of *Mousiké* imitated the modes of action
with singular directness and intimacy. But he does
not analyze either music or the language of lyric
poetry in any of his extant writings. Perhaps the
relevant passages are lost, for the texts of both the
*Politics* and the *Poetics* are incomplete.

One may, however, find the basis for an Aristotelian analysis of lyric language in some parts of
the *Rhetoric*, and in Chapters XXI and XXII of
the *Poetics*. I am thinking especially of his brief
remarks on analogy and metaphor, which he regards
as the basis of poetic language (XXII.9): "But the
greatest thing by far is to have a command of
metaphor. This alone cannot be imparted by
another; it is the mark of genius, for to make good
metaphors implies an eye for resemblances." His
analysis of kinds of metaphors is dull, and he never
demonstrates the coherent metaphors in a whole
poem, as modern critics of lyric verse do; yet the
basic conception is there. His definition of analogy
is austere (XXI.6): "Analogy or proportion is
when the second term is to the first as the fourth
to the third. We may then use the fourth for the
second, or the second for the fourth." But this
conception of analogy has also proved fertile, far
beyond what Aristotle could have foreseen. It is the
basis of the subtle medieval lore of analogy, which
underlies the poetry of Dante's *Divine Comedy*.

The Choral Odes in *Oedipus* may, like all lyrics,
be analyzed in terms of metaphor and analogy.
Take for example the first Strophe of the Parode,
as translated by Fitts and Fitzgerald:

What is the god singing in his profound
Delphi of gold and shadow?
What oracle for Thebes, the sunwhipped city?

Fear unjoints me, the roots of my heart tremble.

Now I remember, O Healer, your power and wonder:
Will you send doom like a sudden cloud, or weave it
Like nightfall of the past?

Ah no: be merciful, issue of holy sound:
Dearest to our expectancy: be tender!

The main metaphors here are of light and darkness:
"gold and shadow," "sunwhipped city," "sudden
cloud," "nightfall of the past." In the rest of the
Ode light and darkness appear in many other
metaphors, and are associated with Apollo, the god
of light, of healing, and also of disease; it was he
who spoke through the Oracle of Delphi. The
imagery of light and darkness runs through the
whole play, stemming from Tiresias's blindness, and
Oedipus's blindness at the end. It is based on the
*analogy* between the eye of the body and the eye
of the mind—sight : blindness :: insight : ignorance.
We may then, as Aristotle points out, use the fourth
term (ignorance) for the second (blindness), and
vice versa. Physical blindness and the darkness of
nightfall express the seeking-action of the play, the
movement-of-spirit from ignorance to insight. The
Chorus "shares in the action," as Aristotle puts it.
The Chorus cannot *do* anything to advance the
quest, but as it suffers its passions of fear and pity
it can grope through associated images of light
and darkness, healing and disease, life and death,
toward the perception of the truth.

It is not my intention, however, to attempt a full
analysis of the poetic language of *Oedipus Rex*. I

merely wish to suggest that, with the aid of the Aristotelian notions of metaphor and analogy, one can see how the Odes also imitate the action. The same principles apply to the poetic language of any good play, and the best modern critics (experts in the lyric) have made such analyses of the language of poetic drama, from Shakespeare to Yeats and Eliot.

## SONG AND SPECTACLE; ACTION AND ACTING

The three basic parts of the art of tragedy are, as we have seen, plot-making, character delineation, and thought-and-language, for by these means the poet gives the action its tragic form, and its concrete actuality. The other three parts, *speech*, in the sense of the art of delivery, *song*, and *spectacle*, all have to do with the production of the play. They are thus essential to the art of tragedy, but concern the poet less directly than the other three, and Aristotle has little to say about them. He apparently did not feel qualified to discuss music and its performance (as one gathers from his remarks on *Mousiké* in *Politics*, VIII), and he seems to have had a low opinion of theatrical production in his time. When he wrote, the great dramatists were gone; and he seems to have known a number of egoistic actors, like some of our modern stars, who made the plays into vehicles for their own personalities.

But Aristotle knew that the poet, in the very act of making his tragedy, had to be an actor. The poet does not need the techniques of voice, diction, and bodily movement, but he must, as he writes, imitate each character in his own inner being and "believe" the situations, just as a good actor does. For tragedy, as he says in his basic definition, is "in the form of actions," i.e., acted by characters. In Chapter XVII.1 and 2, he gives the poet some practical suggestions about achieving this essential quality:

In constructing the plot and working it out with the proper diction, the poet should place the scene, as far as possible, before his eyes. . . . Again, the poet should work out his play, to the best of his power, with appropriate gestures; for those who feel emotion are most convincing through natural sympathy with the characters they represent; and one who is agitated storms, one who is angry rages, with the most lifelike reality. Hence poetry implies either a happy gift of nature, or a strain of madness. In the one case a man can take the mold of any character; in the other, he is lifted out of his proper self.

The purpose of any good technique of acting is to help the actor to perceive the action of the character he is portraying, and then re-create it in his own thought and feeling, as Aristotle says the playwright must do. The best-known acting technique of this kind is that of the Moscow Art Theater, which is widely cultivated (in several versions) in this country. The late Jacques Copeau taught such a technique, and so did the best theater schools in Germany, before Hitler. Each school tends, unfortunately, to develop its own technical vocabulary, but I think their basic assumptions may all be expressed in Aristotelian terms. They all assume that the actor's art consists in "taking the mold" of the character to be portrayed, and then responding to the situations of the play as they appear to that character. Only in that way can the actor

achieve "lifelike reality." Superficial mimicry cannot produce psychological truth, fidelity to the
playwright's imagined people and situations, or
emotional effect on the audience. The masters of
acting technique have a subtle and practical lore of
action. There is no better way to understand
"action," as that concept is used in Aristotle's
*Poetics*, than by studying its practical utility in the
art of acting.

## IV. THE END OF TRAGEDY: PLEASURE, THE UNIVERSAL, AND THE PURGATION OF THE PASSIONS OF FEAR AND PITY

The question why tragedy, with its images of
conflict, terror and suffering, should give us pleasure and satisfaction, has been answered in many
ways. Aristotle's answers, cautious and descriptive
as they are, have interested his readers more than
anything else in the *Poetics*, and produced more
heated controversies among his interpreters. The
appeal of tragedy is in the last analysis inexplicable,
rooted as it is in our mysterious human nature,
but Aristotle's observations of the effect which
tragedy has upon us are as illuminating as anything
we have on the subject.

He accepted, to begin with, the Greek notion
that the fine arts have no end beyond themselves.
The useful arts, shipbuilding, carpentry, and the
like, provide transportation or shelter, but a play or
a symphony cannot be used for anything but
"pleasure." And we have seen that in his introduc-
tory remarks Aristotle suggests that the arts give

pleasure because they satisfy the instincts, or needs, of "imitation" and of "harmony" and "rhythm."

When we recognize the movement-of-spirit "imitated" in a play or poem, we get the satisfaction of knowledge and understanding. The joy of Romeo when he hears Juliet's voice saying his name, the despair of Macbeth when he sees that his mad race is lost, seem to confirm something we half-knew already. The creatures of the poet's imagination do not literally represent anything in our own experience; it must be that *through* word, character, and situation we glimpse something common to men in all times and places. That is why Aristotle writes, (IX.3): "Poetry . . . is a more philosophical and a higher thing than history: for poetry tends to express the universal, history the particular."

"Harmony and rhythm" must refer, not only to music, but to the accords and correspondences that we enjoy in any beautifully formed work of art. Stephen Daedalus, in Joyce's *Portrait of the Artist as a Young Man*, explaining his own Aristotelian conception of art, offers a general definition of rhythm: "Rhythm is the first formal esthetic relation of part to part in any esthetic whole or of an esthetic whole to its part or parts or of any part to the esthetic whole of which it is a part." Young Stephen's formula is laughably pedantic, but (if one thinks it out) extremely accurate. Stephen's whole discussion shows the right way to use Aristotle's ideas: as guides in one's own thinking about art.

Why do harmony and rhythm please us? We do not know; we can only note that they do. "There seems to be in us a sort of affinity to musical modes and rhythms," says Aristotle (*Politics*, VIII), "which makes some philosophers say that the soul is a tuning, others that it possesses tuning." The notion of the human psyche as itself a harmony and rhythm reappears again and again in our tradition, notably in Shakespeare, who often uses music to suggest the health of the inner being.

Such are the pleasures we find in all the fine arts; but the special quality of our pleasure in tragedy may be more closely defined. It comes, says Aristotle, from the purgation of the passions of fear and pity. At this point Stephen's meditations may help us again: "Aristotle has not defined pity and terror. I have. . . . Pity is the feeling which arrests the mind in the presence of whatsoever is grave and constant in human sufferings and unites it with the human sufferer. Terror is the feeling which arrests the mind in the presence of whatsoever is grave and constant in human sufferings and unites it with the secret cause." Notice that these passions must be stirred by the grave and *constant*. A particular calamity with no general meaning—a street accident for example—does not produce the tragic emotion, but only meaningless pain. Here we meet once more the universality of art: the passions of tragedy must spring from something of more than individual, more than momentary, significance. Moreover, the cause of our terror must be "secret." Tragedy, like the Dionysian ceremonies from which it was derived, touches the dark edge of human experience, celebrates a mystery of our nature and destiny.

It would seem (on thinking over the effects of a few tragedies) that pity and fear *together* are required. Pity alone is merely sentimental, like the shameless tears of soap opera. Fear alone, such as we get from a good thriller, merely makes us shift tensely to the edge of the seat and brace ourselves for the pistol shot. But the masters of tragedy, like good cooks, mingle pity and fear in the right proportions. Having given us fear enough, they melt us with pity, purging us of our emotions, and reconciling us to our fate, because we understand it as the universal human lot.

Aristotle's word for this effect is "purgation" or "catharsis." The Greek word can mean either the cleansing of the body (a medical term) or the cleansing of the spirit (a religious term). Some interpreters are shocked by it, because they do not wish to associate poetry with laxatives and enemas; others insist that Aristotle had the religious meaning in mind. I think it is more sensible to assume that Aristotle did not mean either one *literally:* he was talking about tragedy, not medicine or religion, and his use of the term "purgation" is analogical. There are certainly bodily changes (in our chemistry, breathing, muscular tensions, and the like) as we undergo the emotions of tragedy, and they may well constitute a release *like* that of literal purgation. But tragedy speaks essentially to the mind and the spirit, and its effect is *like* that which believers get from religious ceremonies intended to cleanse the spirit. Aristotle noticed (Politics, VIII) that, in religious rituals that he knew, the passions were stirred, released, and at last appeased; and he must have been thinking partly of that when he used the term "purgation" to describe the effect of tragedy.

In the *Poetics* Aristotle does not try to show how the various effects which the art of tragedy aims at, as its "end," are united in an actual play. The pleasures of imitation, harmony, and rhythm; the universal quality of art, and the release and cleansing of the passions, are things he observed, and mentioned in different contexts. But we may, if we like, confirm them in any good tragedy. The effect of *Oedipus Rex*, for example, depends upon its subtle and manifold "rhythm" as Joyce defines the word; upon the pity and fear which are stirred in us, and upon our recognition, at the end, of something both mysterious and universal in Oedipus's fate. Aristotle had a consistent and far-reaching conception of the art of tragedy, and of its end; but his conception only emerges gradually as one thinks over his observations in the light of one's own experience of drama.

## V. THE POETICS AND THE RITUAL FORMS OF GREEK TRAGEDY

For the last hundred years or more, Greek tragedy has been understood as an outgrowth of rites celebrated annually at the Festival of Dionysus. Those rites have been investigated both in their relation to the god Dionysus and in their relation to the primitive religion of the Greeks. The result is a conception of Greek tragedy which is very different from that which prevailed from the Renaissance into the eighteenth century. The Renaissance humanists and their successors saw it in "civilized" and rational terms; in our time we see that much of its form and meaning is due to its primitive source, and to the religious Festival of which it was a part.

This new conception of Greek tragedy has had a very wide effect upon our understanding of the sources of poetry in our tradition, and also upon modern poetry itself, including the theater and music. One thinks of Wagner, and of Nietzsche, who when he wrote *The Birth of Tragedy from the Spirit of Music* was the prophet of Wagner; of Stravinsky, of T. S. Eliot; of French writers as different as Cocteau and Valéry.

In writing the *Poetics* Aristotle was interested in the fully developed tragic form, and not in its ritual sources. He recognized them, however, in his account (IV.12) of the growth of tragedy from the dithyramb. The "quantitative parts" of the tragic plot which he describes are apparently traditional, and derived from the parts of the old rituals. And the "end" of tragedy as he describes it, the purgation of passion, and the embodiment of a universal truth, are analogous to the purposes of religious ritual. The rituals of the Festival of Dionysus are supposed to have included initiation ceremonies, intended to purify the neophyte by the enactment of symbolic ordeals and sacrifices; and also "rites of spring," symbolic enactments of the death and rebirth of a "season-spirit" (as Harrison calls him), upon whom the annual renewal of vegetable life was thought to depend. If these modern theories of the ritual sources of tragedy do not explain the *Poetics* directly, they may throw light upon it indirectly, by deepening our understanding of the art form which Aristotle was analyzing.

Unfortunately little is known directly about the rites of the Dionysian Festival, or about the poets, Aeschylus's predecessors, who gradually made the tragic form out of ritual. The scholars who devote their lives to such matters do not agree upon the evidence to be accepted, nor upon the interpretation of the evidence. But some of their theories are extremely suggestive, especially those of the Cambridge school, Frazer (of *The Golden Bough*), Cornford, Harrison, Murray, and their colleagues and followers. It is this school which has had the deepest influence upon modern poetry and upon the whole climate of ideas in which we now read Greek tragedy and the *Poetics*.

Jane Ellen Harrison's *Themis, A Study of the Social Origins of Greek Religion,* is a basic work of this school. It contains a note by Gilbert Murray on "The Ritual Forms Preserved in Greek Tragedy." Murray writes (page 341):

The following note presupposes certain general views about the origin and essential nature of Greek Tragedy. It assumes that Tragedy is in origin a Ritual Dance. . . . Further, it assumes, in accord with the overwhelming weight of ancient tradition, that the dance in question is originally or centrally that of Dionysus; and it regards Dionysus, in this connection, as the spirit of the Dithyramb or Spring Drômenon . . . an "Eniautos-Daimon" [Season-Spirit] who represents the cyclical death and rebirth of the world, including the rebirth of the tribe by the return of the heroes or dead ancestors.

Murray is referring to such mythic figures as Attis, Adonis, and Osiris, whose cults and legends are described by Frazer in *The Golden Bough;* representatives of the Season-Spirit. Murray continues:

If we examine the kind of myth which seems to underlie the various "Eniautos" celebrations we shall find:

1. An *Agon* or Contest, the Year against its enemy, Light against Darkness, Summer against Winter.

2. A *Pathos* of the Year-Daimon, generally a ritual or sacrificial death, in which Adonis or Attis is slain by

the tabu animal, the Pharmakos stoned, Osiris, Dionysus, Pentheus, Orpheus, Hippolytus torn to pieces (sparagmos).

3. A *Messenger*. For this Pathos seems seldom or never to be actually performed under the eye of the audience. . . . It is announced by a messenger.

4. A *Threnos* or Lamentation. Specially characteristic, however, is a clash of contrary emotions, the death of the old being also the triumph of the new. . . .

5 and 6. An *Anagnorisis*—discovery or recognition—of the slain and mutilated Daimon, followed by his Resurrection or Apotheosis or, in some sense, his "Epiphany in glory." . . . It naturally goes with a *Peripeteia* or extreme change of feeling from grief to joy.

Murray does not maintain that the ancient rituals were all exactly the same, nor that the Greek tragedies we have exactly follow any ritual pattern. He lists all of the extant tragedies, and briefly indicates the ritual forms which he finds, in a different way, in each one.

The theory here expounded by Murray has been much criticized by other experts, and the whole field is full of disputes so erudite that the non-specialist can only look on in respectful silence. But the general notion—that the ritual enactment of struggle, suffering, sacrifice, and the appearance of new light and new life, is at the root of the tragic form—is an insight of the first importance. In primitive societies the ritual is intended to assure the rebirth of vegetation, upon which the physical life of the tribe depends, after the annual death of winter. In civilized societies it comes to signify the rebirth of the human spirit through suffering, as in the Christian liturgy. In *Oedipus Rex* many very primitive elements are present: the wasting of the

| Oedipus Rex (sequence of scenes) | Action of Play | "Quantitative Parts" Poetics XII | "Organic Parts" Poetics X, XI | Parts of the Dionysian Ritual (after Murray) |
|---|---|---|---|---|
| Citizens ask Oedipus for help, Creon brings word from the Oracle | To discover how to cure Thebes of plague | Prologue | | (a Messenger often gives a Prologue—cf. Creon in the play) |
| chorus | | Parode | | |
| Oedipus and Tiresias | To find the slayer of Laius (rational purpose) | Episodes and Choric Songs | | Agon or Contest, season-spirit against its antagonists |
| chorus | | | | |
| Oedipus and Creon | | | | |
| Oedipus, Creon, Jocasta | | | | |
| Oedipus with chorus | | commos | | |
| Oedipus and Jocasta | | Episodes and Choric Song | Reversal and Recognition | Anagnorisis or Recognition and Threnos or Lamentation |
| chorus | | | | |
| Jocasta, Messenger, Oedipus | | | | |
| chorus with Oedipus | | commos | | |
| Oedipus and Shepherd | | Episode and Choric Song | | |
| chorus | | | | |
| Attendant, Chorus, Oedipus Blind, Creon | To accept the truth (Pathos—Perception) | Exode | Pathos or "Scene of Suffering" | Pathos, with Messenger (in the play, above, the Attendant who tells of Jocasta's death and Oedipus' blinding.) |
| Chorus alone (final lines) | | | | Epiphany |

The relation between the scenes of *Oedipus Rex*, the action of the play, the "parts" of the play according to Aristotle, and the parts of the Ritual according to Murray.

40

physical life of Thebes under its "plague," Oedipus's limp, and his mutilated eyes, signs characteristic of the scapegoat, king, or semidivine hero,
who undergoes ritual combat and suffering to re-
store the life of the community. But in Sophocles'
play these ancient savage elements represent the renewal, or cleansing, of the life of the spirit through
suffering and the perception of truth.

The table on page 40 is intended to show parallels
between the form of *Oedipus Rex*, as Aristotle
analyzes the tragic form, and the ritual forms as
reconstructed by Murray and his school. It is
offered, not as a provable or disprovable hypothesis,
but as an "aid to reflection" upon the form and
meaning of tragedy.

## Suggestions for Further Reading

This short list is confined to books in English,
most of them easily available in libraries or in in-
expensive editions. The reader who wishes to go
farther into the vast literature on the *Poetics* and
related topics will find bibliographies in several of
the books listed below.

Books available in paperback editions are marked
with an asterisk [*].

### I. THE POETICS IN ENGLISH

S. H. Butcher. *Aristotle's Theory of Poetry and
Fine Art.* 4th ed., London: 1932. Contains our
text in Greek and English, with a long essay by
Butcher.

Ingram Bywater. *Aristotle on the Art of Poetry.*

Oxford: 1909. The other most respected text in English.

Gerald F. Else. *Aristotle's Poetics: The Argument*. Cambridge, Mass., 1957. This work, which runs to more than 650 pages, is the latest study of the *Poetics*. It is a valuable reference book on textual problems and on many controversial questions of interpretation.

## II. OTHER WORKS OF ARISTOTLE REFERRED TO IN THE INTRODUCTION

Philip Wheelwright. *Aristotle*. New York: 1951. Important passages from seven works of Aristotle, including *Nicomachean Ethics*, *Poetics*, *Psychology*, and *Politics* (with the passage on Music, Chapter VIII), "Selected and translated from the original Greek into the English of today by Philip Wheelwright."

Ernest Barker. *The Politics of Aristotle*.\* New York: 1958.

J. A. K. Thomson. *The Ethics of Aristotle*.\* London: 1953.

W. Rhys Roberts. *Aristotle, Rhetorica*, in Vol. XI, Oxford Translations. Oxford: 1924.

## III. THE POETICS IN LITERARY THEORY AND CRITICISM

J. E. Spingarn. *A History of Literary Criticism in the Renaissance*. New York: 1938. A standard account of theories of literature in the sixteenth and seventeenth centuries, when the *Poetics* was generally regarded as the basic work on the subject.

Ronald S. Crane *et al. Critics and Criticism Ancient and Modern.* Chicago: 1952. As Professor Crane explains in his Introduction, a "major concern of the essays here collected is with the capacities for modern development and use . . . of the poetic method of Aristotle."

Kenneth Burke. *Counterstatement.** New York: 1957. The best introduction to Mr. Burke's theory of literature, which is based on the Aristotelian concept of action.

Jacques Maritain. *Creative Intuition in Art and Poetry.** New York: 1955. A basic work on the creative process, with reference to the theory of poetry since Baudelaire, and also to the Aristotelian concept of action.

Francis Fergusson. *The Idea of a Theatre.** New York: 1953. A study of ten representative plays, from Sophocles to Eliot, as "imitations" of different modes of action.

IV. RITUAL FORMS OF GREEK TRAGEDY:
BOOKS MENTIONED IN THE ESSAY

Friedrich Nietzsche. *The Birth of Tragedy,* and *The Genealogy of Morals.** New York: 1956.

Jane Ellen Harrison. *Themis: A Study of the Social Origins of Greek Religion.* With an Excursus on the Ritual Forms Preserved in Greek Tragedy, by Professor Gilbert Murray, and a Chapter on the "Origins of the Olympic Games" by Mr. F. M. Cornford. Cambridge: 1912.

### V. TRANSLATIONS OF "OEDIPUS REX"

Dudley Fitts and Robert Fitzgerald. *The Oedipus Cycle of Sophocles.** New York: 1955.

Bernard M. W. Knox. *Oedipus the King.** New York: 1959.

FRANCIS FERGUSSON

# ARISTOTLE'S *POETICS*

## ANALYSIS OF CONTENTS

I. "Imitation" ($\mu\dot{\iota}\mu\eta\sigma\iota\varsigma$) the common principle of the Arts of Poetry, Music, Dancing, Painting, and Sculpture. These Arts distinguished according to the Medium or material Vehicle, the Objects, and the Manner of Imitation. The Medium of Imitation is Rhythm, Language, and "Harmony" (or Melody), taken singly or combined.

II. The Objects of Imitation.

Higher or lower types are represented in all the Imitative Arts. In Poetry this is the basis of the distinction between Tragedy and Comedy.

III. The Manner of Imitation.

Poetry may be in form either dramatic narrative, pure narrative (including lyric poetry), or pure drama. A digression follows on the name and original home of the Drama.

IV. The Origin and Development of Poetry.

Psychologically, Poetry may be traced to two causes, the instinct of Imitation, and the instinct of "Harmony" and Rhythm.

Historically viewed, Poetry diverged early in two directions: traces of this twofold tendency are found in the Homeric poems; Tragedy and Comedy exhibit the distinction in a developed form.

The successive steps in the history of Tragedy are enumerated.

V. Definition of the Ludicrous ($\tau\dot{o}$ $\gamma\epsilon\lambda o\hat{\iota}o\nu$), and a brief sketch of the rise of Comedy. Points of comparison between Epic Poetry and Tragedy. (The chapter is fragmentary.)

**VI.** Definition of Tragedy. Six elements in Tragedy: three external—namely, Spectacular Presentment (ὁ τῆς ὄψεως κόσμος or ὄψις), Lyrical Song (μελοποιία), Diction (λέξις); three internal—namely, Plot (μῦθος), Character (ἦθος), and Thought (διάνοια). Plot, or the representation of the action, is of primary importance; Character and Thought come next in order.

**VII.** The Plot must be a Whole, complete in itself, and of adequate magnitude.

**VIII.** The Plot must be a Unity. Unity of Plot consists not in Unity of Hero, but in Unity of Action.

The parts must be organically connected.

**IX.** (Plot continued.) Dramatic Unity can be attained only by the observance of Poetic as distinct from Historic Truth; for Poetry is an expression of the Universal, History of the Particular. The rule of probable or necessary sequence as applied to the incidents. Certain plots condemned for want of Unity.

The best Tragic effects depend on the combination of the Inevitable and the Unexpected.

**X.** (Plot continued.) Definitions of Simple (ἁπλοῖ) and Complex (πεπλεγμένοι) Plots.

**XI.** (Plot continued.) Reversal of the Situation (περιπέτεια), Recognition (ἀναγνώρισις), and Tragic or disastrous Incident (πάθος) defined and explained.

**XII.** The "quantitative parts" (μέρη κατὰ τὸ ποσόν) of Tragedy defined: Prologue, Episode, etc. (Probably an interpolation.)

**XIII.** (Plot continued.) What constitutes Tragic Action. The change of fortune and the character of the hero as requisite to an ideal Tragedy. The unhappy ending more truly tragic than the "poetic justice" which is in

favor with a popular audience, and belongs
rather to Comedy.

XIV. (Plot continued.) The tragic emotions of pity
and fear should spring out of the Plot itself.
To produce them by Scenery or Spectacular
effect is entirely against the spirit of Tragedy. Examples of Tragic Incidents designed
to heighten the emotional effect.

XV. The element of Character (as the manifestation
of moral purpose) in Tragedy. Requisites of
ethical portraiture. The rule of necessity or
probability applicable to Character as to Plot.
The "Deus ex Machina" (a passage out of
place here). How Character is idealized.

XVI. (Plot continued.) Recognition: its various
kinds, with examples.

XVII. Practical rules for the Tragic Poet:
(1) To place the scene before his eyes,
and to act the parts himself in order to enter
into vivid sympathy with the *dramatis personae.*
(2) To sketch the bare outline of the action before proceeding to fill in the episodes.
The Episodes of Tragedy are here in-
cidentally contrasted with those of Epic
Poetry.

XVIII. Further rules for the Tragic Poet:
(1) To be careful about the Complication
(δέσις) and Denouement (λύσις) of the Plot,
especially the Denouement.
(2) To unite, if possible, varied forms of
poetic excellence.
(3) Not to overcharge a Tragedy with details appropriate to Epic Poetry.
(4) To make the Choral Odes—like the
Dialogue—an organic part of the whole.

XIX. Thought (διάνοια), or the Intellectual element,
and Diction in Tragedy.
Thought is revealed in the dramatic
speeches composed according to the rules of
Rhetoric.

S. H. BUTCHER

# I

I PROPOSE TO TREAT OF
Poetry in itself and of its various kinds, noting the
essential quality of each; to inquire into the structure of the plot as requisite to a good poem; into
the number and nature of the parts of which a poem
is composed; and similarly into whatever else falls
within the same inquiry. Following, then, the order
of nature, let us begin with the principles which
come first.

Epic poetry and Tragedy, Comedy also and 2
Dithyrambic poetry, and the music of the flute and
of the lyre in most of their forms, are all in their
general conception modes of imitation. They differ, 3
however, from one another in three respects—the
medium, the objects, the manner or mode of imitation, being in each case distinct.

For as there are persons who, by conscious art or 4
mere habit, imitate and represent various objects
through the medium of color and form, or again by

the voice, so in the arts above mentioned, taken as a whole, the imitation is produced by rhythm, language, or "harmony," either singly or combined.

Thus in the music of the flute and of the lyre, "harmony" and rhythm alone are employed; also in other arts, such as that of the shepherd's pipe, which are essentially similar to these. In dancing, rhythm 5 alone is used without "harmony," for even dancing imitates character, emotion, and action, by rhythmical movement.

There is another art which imitates by means of 6 language alone, and that either in prose or verse—which verse, again, may either combine different meters or consist of but one kind—but this has hitherto been without a name. For there is no com- 7 mon term we could apply to the mimes of Sophron and Xenarchus and the Socratic dialogues on the one hand; and, on the other, to poetic imitations in iambic, elegiac, or any similar meter. People do, indeed, add the word "maker" or "poet" to the name of the meter, and speak of elegiac poets, or epic (that is, hexameter) poets, as if it were not the imitation that makes the poet, but the verse that entitles them all indiscriminately to the name. Even 8 when a treatise on medicine or natural science is brought out in verse, the name of poet is by custom given to the author; and yet Homer and Empedocles have nothing in common but the meter, so that it would be right to call the one poet, the other physicist rather than poet. On the same principle, 9 even if a writer in his poetic imitation were to combine all meters, as Chaeremon did in his *Centaur*, which is a medley composed of meters of all kinds, we should bring him too under the general term poet. So much then for these distinctions.

There are, again, some arts which employ all the 10 means above mentioned—namely, rhythm, tune, and meter. Such are Dithyrambic and Nomic poetry, and also Tragedy and Comedy; but between them the difference is that in the first two cases these means are all employed in combination, in the latter, now one means is employed, now another.

Such, then, are the differences of the arts with respect to the medium of imitation.

# II

SINCE THE OBJECTS OF IMI-
tation are men in action, and these men must be
either of a higher or a lower type (for moral
character mainly answers to these divisions, goodness and badness being the distinguishing marks
of moral differences), it follows that we must represent men either as better than in real life, or as
worse, or as they are. It is the same in painting.
Polygnotus depicted men as nobler than they are,
Pauson as less noble, Dionysius drew them true to
life.

Now it is evident that each of the modes of imita- 2
tion above mentioned will exhibit these differences,
and become a distinct kind in imitating objects that
are thus distinct. Such diversities may be found 3
even in dancing, flute-playing, and lyre-playing. So
again in language, whether prose or verse unaccom-
panied by music. Homer, for example, makes men
better than they are; Cleophon as they are;
Hegemon the Thasian, the inventor of parodies,
and Nicochares, the author of the *Deiliad*, worse
than they are. The same thing holds good of Dithy- 4
rambs and Nomes; here too one may portray different types, as Timotheus and Philoxenus differed
in representing their Cyclopes. The same distinction marks off Tragedy from Comedy; for Comedy
aims at representing men as worse, Tragedy as
better than in actual life.

# III

THERE IS STILL A THIRD DIF-
ference—the manner in which each of these objects
may be imitated. For the medium being the same,
and the objects the same, the poet may imitate by
narration—in which case he either take another
personality as Homer does, or speak in his own
person, unchanged—or he may present all his
characters as living and moving before us.

These, then, as we said at the beginning, are the 2
three differences which distinguish artistic imitation
—the medium, the objects, and the manner. So that,
from one point of view, Sophocles is an imitator of
the same kind as Homer—for both imitate higher
types of character; from another point of view, of
the same kind as Aristophanes—for both imitate
persons acting and doing. Hence, some say, the 3
name of "drama" is given to such poems, as representing action. For the same reason the Dorians
claim the invention both of Tragedy and Comedy.

The claim to Comedy is put forward by the Megarians—not only by those of Greece proper, who
allege that it originated under their democracy, but
also by the Megarians of Sicily, for the poet Epi-
charmus, who is much earlier than Chionides and
Magnes, belonged to that country. Tragedy too is
claimed by certain Dorians of the Peloponnese. In
each case they appeal to the evidence of language.
The outlying villages, they say, are by them called
κῶμαι, by the Athenians δῆμοι: and they assume that
Comedians were so named not from κωμάζειν, "to
revel," but because they wandered from village to
village (κατὰ κώμας), being excluded contemptuously
from the city. They add also that the Dorian word
for "doing" is δρᾶν, and the Athenian, πράττειν.

This may suffice as to the number and nature of [4]
the various modes of imitation.

# IV

POETRY IN GENERAL SEEMS
to have sprung from two causes, each of them lying
deep in our nature. First, the instinct of imitation is 2
implanted in man from childhood, one difference
between him and other animals being that he is the
most imitative of living creatures, and through
imitation learns his earliest lessons; and no less universal is the pleasure felt in things imitated. We 3
have evidence of this in the facts of experience.
Objects which in themselves we view with pain, we
delight to contemplate when reproduced with
minute fidelity: such as the forms of the most
ignoble animals and of dead bodies. The cause of 4
this again is that to learn gives the liveliest pleasure,
not only to philosophers but to men in general;
whose capacity, however, of learning is more
limited. Thus the reason why men enjoy seeing a 5
likeness is that in contemplating it they find themselves learning or inferring, and saying perhaps,

"Ah, that is he." For if you happen not to have seen the original, the pleasure will be due not to the imitation as such, but to the execution, the coloring, or some such other cause.

Imitation, then, is one instinct of our nature. Next, 6 there is the instinct for "harmony" and rhythm, meters being manifestly sections of rhythm. Persons, therefore, starting with this natural gift developed by degrees their special aptitudes, till their rude improvisations gave birth to Poetry.

Poetry now diverged in two directions, according 7 to the individual character of the writers. The graver spirits imitated noble actions, and the actions of good men. The more trivial sort imitated the actions of meaner persons, at first composing satires, as the former did hymns to the gods and the praises of famous men. A poem of the satirical kind cannot 8 indeed be put down to any author earlier than Homer; though many such writers probably there were. But from Homer onward, instances can be cited—his own *Margites*, for example, and other similar compositions. The appropriate meter was also here introduced; hence the measure is still called the iambic or lampooning measure, being that in which people lampooned one another. Thus the 9 older poets were distinguished as writers of heroic or of lampooning verse.

As, in the serious style, Homer is pre-eminent among poets, for he alone combined dramatic form with excellence of imitation, so he too first laid down the main lines of Comedy, by dramatizing the ludicrous instead of writing personal satire. His *Margites* bears the same relation to Comedy that the *Iliad* and *Odyssey* do to Tragedy. But when 10 Tragedy and Comedy came to light, the two classes of poets still followed their natural bent: the lampooners became writers of Comedy, and the Epic poets were succeeded by Tragedians, since the drama was a larger and higher form of art.

Whether Tragedy has as yet perfected its proper 11 types or not, and whether it is to be judged in itself, or in relation also to the audience—this raises another question. Be that as it may, Tragedy—as also 12 Comedy—was at first mere improvisation. The one originated with the authors of the Dithyramb, the other with those of the phallic songs, which are still in use in many of our cities. Tragedy advanced by slow degrees; each new element that showed itself was in turn developed. Having passed through many changes, it found its natural form, and there it stopped.

Aeschylus first introduced a second actor; he 13 diminished the importance of the Chorus, and assigned the leading part to the dialogue. Sophocles raised the number of actors to three, and added scene-painting. Moreover, it was not till late that 14 the short plot was discarded for one of greater compass, and the grotesque diction of the earlier satyric form for the stately manner of Tragedy. The iambic measure then replaced the trochaic tetrameter, which was originally employed when the poetry was of the satyric order, and had greater affinities with dancing. Once dialogue had come in, Nature herself discovered the appropriate measure. For the iambic is, of all measures, the most colloquial: we see it in the fact that conversational speech runs into iambic lines more frequently than into any other kind of verse; rarely into hexameters, and only when we drop the colloquial intonation. The additions to the number of "episodes" or acts, 15 and the other accessories of which tradition tells, must be taken as already described; for to discuss them in detail would, doubtless, be a large undertaking.

# V

COMEDY IS, AS WE HAVE said, an imitation of characters of a lower type— not, however, in the full sense of the word bad, the Ludicrous being merely a subdivision of the ugly. It consists in some defect or ugliness which is not painful or destructive. To take an obvious example, the comic mask is ugly and distorted, but does not imply pain.

The successive changes through which Tragedy [2] passed, and the authors of these changes, are well known, whereas Comedy has had no history, because it was not at first treated seriously. It was late before the Archon granted a comic chorus to a poet; the performers were till then voluntary. Comedy had already taken definite shape when comic poets, distinctively so called, are heard of. Who furnished it with masks, or prologues, or in- [3] creased the number of actors—these and other similar details remain unknown. As for the plot, it came originally from Sicily; but of Athenian writers Crates was the first who, abandoning the "iambic" or lampooning form, generalized his themes and plots.

Epic poetry agrees with Tragedy in so far as it is 4 an imitation in verse of characters of a higher type. They differ, in that Epic poetry admits but one kind of meter, and is narrative in form. They differ, again, in their length: for Tragedy endeavors, as far as possible, to confine itself to a single revolution of the sun, or but slightly to exceed this limit; whereas the Epic action has no limits of time. This, then, is a second point of difference, though at first the same freedom was admitted in Tragedy as in Epic poetry.

Of their constituent parts some are common to 5 both, some peculiar to Tragedy: whoever, therefore, knows what is good or bad Tragedy, knows also about Epic poetry. All the elements of an Epic poem are found in Tragedy, but the elements of a Tragedy are not all found in the Epic poem.

# VI

Of the poetry which imi-
tates in hexameter verse, and of Comedy, we will
speak hereafter. Let us now discuss Tragedy, resum-
ing its formal definition, as resulting from what has
been already said.

Tragedy, then, is an imitation of an action that is 2
serious, complete, and of a certain magnitude; in
language embellished with each kind of artistic
ornament, the several kinds being found in separate
parts of the play; in the form of action, not of
narrative; through pity and fear effecting the proper
purgation of these emotions. By "language embel- 3
lished," I mean language into which rhythm,
"harmony," and song enter. By "the several kinds
in separate parts," I mean that some parts are
rendered through the medium of verse alone, others
again with the aid of song.

Now as tragic imitation implies persons acting, it 4
necessarily follows, in the first place, that Spectacu-

lar equipment will be a part of Tragedy. Next, Song and Diction, for these are the medium of imitation. By "Diction" I mean the mere metrical arrangement of the words: as for "Song," it is a term whose sense everyone understands.

Again, Tragedy is the imitation of an action; and 5 an action implies personal agents, who necessarily possess certain distinctive qualities both of character and thought; for it is by these that we qualify actions themselves, and these—thought and character —are the two natural causes from which actions spring, and on actions again all success or failure depends. Hence, the Plot is the imitation of the action: 6 for by plot I here mean the arrangement of the incidents. By Character I mean that in virtue of which we ascribe certain qualities to the agents. Thought is required wherever a statement is proved, or, it may be, a general truth enunciated. Every Tragedy, 7 therefore, must have six parts, which parts determine its quality—namely, Plot, Character, Diction, Thought, Spectacle, Song. Two of the parts constitute the medium of imitation, one the manner, and three the objects of imitation. And these complete the list. These elements have been employed, 8 we may say, by the poets to a man; in fact, every play contains Spectacular elements as well as Character, Plot, Diction, Song, and Thought.

But most important of all is the structure of the 9 incidents. For Tragedy is an imitation, not of men, but of an action and of life, and life consists in action, and its end is a mode of action, not a quality. Now character determines men's qualities, but it is 10 by their actions that they are happy or the reverse. Dramatic action, therefore, is not with a view to the representation of character: character comes in as

subsidiary to the actions. Hence the incidents and
the plot are the end of a tragedy; and the end is the
chief thing of all. Again, without action there can- 11
not be a tragedy; there may be without character.
The tragedies of most of our modern poets fail in
the rendering of character; and of poets in general
this is often true. It is the same in painting; and here
lies the difference between Zeuxis and Polygnotus.
Polygnotus delineates character well: the style of
Zeuxis is devoid of ethical quality. Again, if you 12
string together a set of speeches expressive of character, and well finished in point of diction and
thought, you will not produce the essential tragic
effect nearly so well as with a play which, however
deficient in these respects, yet has a plot and artis-
tically constructed incidents. Besides which, the 13
most powerful elements of emotional interest in
Tragedy—Peripeteia or Reversal of the Situation,
and Recognition scenes—are parts of the plot. A 14
further proof is that novices in the art attain to
finish of diction and precision of portraiture before
they can construct the plot. It is the same with almost all the early poets.

The Plot, then, is the first principle, and, as it
were, the soul of a tragedy: Character holds the
second place. A similar fact is seen in painting. The 15
most beautiful colors, laid on confusedly, will not
give as much pleasure as the chalk outline of a portrait. Thus Tragedy is the imitation of an action, and
of the agents mainly with a view to the action.

Third in order is Thought—that is, the faculty of 16
saying what is possible and pertinent in given circumstances. In the case of oratory, this is the function of the political art and of the art of rhetoric:
and so indeed the older poets make their characters

speak the language of civic life; the poets of our time, the language of the rhetoricians. Character is 17 that which reveals moral purpose, showing what kind of things a man chooses or avoids. Speeches, therefore, which do not make this manifest, or in which the speaker does not choose or avoid anything whatever, are not expressive of character. Thought, on the other hand, is found where something is proved to be or not to be, or a general maxim is enunciated.

Fourth among the elements enumerated comes 18 Diction; by which I mean, as has been already said, the expression of the meaning in words; and its essence is the same both in verse and prose.

Of the remaining elements Song holds the chief 19 place among the embellishments.

The Spectacle has, indeed, an emotional attraction of its own, but, of all the parts, it is the least artistic, and connected least with the art of poetry. For the power of Tragedy, we may be sure, is felt even apart from representation and actors. Besides, the production of spectacular effects depends more on the art of the stage machinist than on that of the poet.

# VII

THESE PRINCIPLES BEING ES-
tablished, let us now discuss the proper structure of
the Plot, since this is the first and most important
thing in Tragedy.

Now, according to our definition, Tragedy is an 2
imitation of an action that is complete, and whole,
and of a certain magnitude; for there may be a
whole that is wanting in magnitude. A whole is that 3
which has a beginning, a middle, and an end. A
beginning is that which does not itself follow anything by causal necessity, but after which something
naturally is or comes to be. An end, on the contrary,
is that which itself naturally follows some other
thing, either by necessity, or as a rule, but has
nothing following it. A middle is that which follows
something as some other thing follows it. A well-
constructed plot, therefore, must neither begin nor
end at haphazard, but conform to these principles.

Again, a beautiful object, whether it be a living 4

organism or any whole composed of parts, must not only have an orderly arrangement of parts, but must also be of a certain magnitude; for beauty depends on magnitude and order. Hence a very small animal organism cannot be beautiful; for the view of it is confused, the object being seen in an almost imperceptible moment of time. Nor, again, can one of vast size be beautiful; for as the eye cannot take it all in at once, the unity and sense of the whole is lost for the spectator; as for instance if there were one a thousand miles long. As, therefore, in the 5 case of animate bodies and organisms a certain magnitude is necessary, and a magnitude which may be easily embraced in one view; so in the plot, a certain length is necessary, and a length which can be easily embraced by the memory. The limit of 6 length in relation to dramatic competition and sensuous presentment is no part of artistic theory. For had it been the rule for a hundred tragedies to compete together, the performance would have been regulated by the water clock—as indeed we are told was formerly done. But the limit as fixed by the 7 nature of the drama itself is this: the greater the length, the more beautiful will the piece be by reason of its size, provided that the whole be perspicuous. And to define the matter roughly, we may say that the proper magnitude is comprised within such limits that the sequence of events, according to the law of probability or necessity, will admit of a change from bad fortune to good, or from good fortune to bad.

# VIII

Unity of plot does not, as some persons think, consist in the unity of the hero. For infinitely various are the incidents in one man's life which cannot be reduced to unity; and so, too, there are many actions of one man out of which we cannot make one action. Hence the error, as it ap- 2 pears, of all poets who have composed a *Heracleid,* a *Theseid,* or other poems of the kind. They imagine that as Heracles was one man, the story of Heracles must also be a unity. But Homer, as in all else he is 3 of surpassing merit, here too—whether from art or natural genius—seems to have happily discerned the truth. In composing the *Odyssey* he did not include all the adventures of Odysseus—such as his wound on Parnassus, or his feigned madness at the muster- ing of the host—incidents between which there was no necessary or probable connection: but he made the *Odyssey,* and likewise the *Iliad,* to center round an action that in our sense of the word is one. As, 4 therefore, in the other imitative arts, the imitation is one when the object imitated is one, so the plot, being an imitation of an action, must imitate one action and that a whole, the structural union of the parts being such that, if any one of them is displaced or removed, the whole will be disjointed and dis- turbed. For a thing whose presence or absence makes no visible difference is not an organic part of the whole.

# IX

IT IS, MOREOVER, EVIDENT from what has been said that it is not the function of the poet to relate what has happened, but what may happen—what is possible according to the law of probability or necessity. The poet and the his- 2 torian differ not by writing in verse or in prose. The work of Herodotus might be put into verse, and it would still be a species of history, with meter no less than without it. The true difference is that one relates what has happened, the other what may happen. Poetry, therefore, is a more philosophical 3 and a higher thing than history: for poetry tends to express the universal, history the particular. By the 4 universal I mean how a person of a certain type will on occasion speak or act, according to the law of probability or necessity; and it is this universality at which poetry aims in the names she attaches to the personages. The particular is—for example— what Alcibiades did or suffered. In Comedy this is 5

already apparent: for here the poet first constructs
the plot on the lines of probability, and then inserts
characteristic names—unlike the lampooners who
write about particular individuals. But tragedians 6
still keep to real names, the reason being that what
is possible is credible: what has not happened we do
not at once feel sure to be possible, but what has
happened is manifestly possible: otherwise it would
not have happened. Still there are even some trage- 7
dies in which there are only one or two well-known
names, the rest being fictitious. In others, none are
well known—as in Agathon's *Antheus*, where incidents and names alike are fictitious, and yet they
give none the less pleasure. We must not, therefore, 8
at all costs keep to the received legends, which are
the usual subjects of Tragedy. Indeed, it would be
absurd to attempt it; for even subjects that are
known are known only to a few, and yet give
pleasure to all. It clearly follows that the poet or 9
"maker" should be the maker of plots rather than
of verses, since he is a poet because he imitates, and
what he imitates are actions. And even if he chances
to take an historical subject, he is none the less a
poet; for there is no reason why some events that
have actually happened should not conform to the
law of the probable and possible, and in virtue of
that quality in them he is their poet or maker.

Of all plots and actions the epeisodic are the 10
worst. I call a plot "epeisodic" in which the episodes
or acts succeed one another without probable or
necessary sequence. Bad poets compose such pieces
by their own fault, good poets, to please the players;
for, as they write show pieces for competition, they
stretch the plot beyond its capacity and are often
forced to break the natural continuity.

But again, Tragedy is an imitation not only of a 11
complete action, but of events inspiring fear or
pity. Such an effect is best produced when the
events come on us by surprise; and the effect is
heightened when, at the same time, they follow as
cause and effect. The tragic wonder will then be 12
greater than if they happened of themselves or by
accident, for even coincidences are most striking
when they have an air of design. We may instance
the statue of Mitys at Argos, which fell upon his
murderer while he was a spectator at a festival, and
killed him. Such events seem not to be due to mere
chance. Plots, therefore, constructed on these
principles are necessarily the best.

# X

PLOTS ARE EITHER SIMPLE
or Complex, for the actions in real life, of which the
plots are an imitation, obviously show a similar
distinction. An action which is one and continuous 2
in the sense above defined, I call Simple, when the
change of fortune takes place without Reversal of
the Situation and without Recognition.

A Complex action is one in which the change is
accompanied by such Reversal, or by Recognition,
or by both. These last should arise from the internal 3
structure of the plot, so that what follows should be
the necessary or probable result of the preceding
action. It makes all the difference whether any given
event is a case of *propter hoc* or *post hoc*.

# XI

Reversal of the Situation
is a change by which the action veers round to its
opposite, subject always to our rule of probability
or necessity. Thus in the *Oedipus*, the messenger
comes to cheer Oedipus and free him from his
alarms about his mother, but by revealing who he is,
he produces the opposite effect. Again in the
*Lynceus*, Lynceus is being led away to his death,
and Danaus goes with him, meaning to slay him;
but the outcome of the preceding incidents is that
Danaus is killed and Lynceus saved.

Recognition, as the name indicates, is a change 2
from ignorance to knowledge, producing love or
hate between the persons destined by the poet for
good or bad fortune. The best form of recognition
is coincident with a Reversal of the Situation, as in
the *Oedipus*. There are indeed other forms. Even 3
inanimate things of the most trivial kind may in a
sense be objects of recognition. Again, we may

recognize or discover whether a person has done a thing or not. But the recognition which is most intimately connected with the plot and action is, as we have said, the recognition of persons. This recog- 4 nition, combined with Reversal, will produce either pity or fear; and actions producing these effects are those which, by our definition, Tragedy represents. Moreover, it is upon such situations that the issues of good or bad fortune will depend. Recognition, 5 then, being between persons, it may happen that one person only is recognized by the other—when the latter is already known—or it may be necessary that the recognition should be on both sides. Thus Iphigenia is revealed to Orestes by the sending of the letter; but another act of recognition is required to make Orestes known to Iphigenia.

Two parts, then, of the Plot—Reversal of the 6 Situation and Recognition—turn upon surprises. A third part is the Scene of Suffering. The Scene of Suffering is a destructive or painful action, such as death on the stage, bodily agony, wounds and the like.

# XII

[THE PARTS OF TRAGEDY
which must be treated as elements of the whole
have been already mentioned. We now come to the
quantitative parts—the separate parts into which
Tragedy is divided—namely, Prologue, Episode,
Exode, Choric song; this last being divided into
Parode and Stasimon. These are common to all
plays; peculiar to some are the songs of actors from
the stage and the Commoi.

The Prologue is that entire part of a tragedy 2
which precedes the Parode of the Chorus. The
Episode is that entire part of a tragedy which is between complete choric songs. The Exode is that
entire part of a tragedy which has no choric song
after it. Of the Choric part the Parode is the first
undivided utterance of the Chorus: the Stasimon is
a Choric ode without anapests or trochaic tetram-
eters: the Commos is a joint lamentation of Chorus
and actors. The parts of Tragedy which must be 3
treated as elements of the whole have been already
mentioned. The quantitative parts—the separate
parts into which it is divided—are here enumerated.]

# XIII

AS THE SEQUEL TO WHAT HAS already been said, we must proceed to consider what the poet should aim at, and what he should avoid, in constructing his plots; and by what means the specific effect of Tragedy will be produced.

A perfect tragedy should, as we have seen, be[2] arranged not on the simple but on the complex plan. It should, moreover, imitate actions which excite pity and fear, this being the distinctive mark of tragic imitation. It follows plainly, in the first place, that the change of fortune presented must not be the spectacle of a virtuous man brought from prosperity to adversity: for this moves neither pity nor fear; it merely shocks us. Nor, again, that of a bad man passing from adversity to prosperity, for nothing can be more alien to the spirit of Tragedy: it possesses no single tragic quality; it neither satisfies the moral sense nor calls forth pity or fear. Nor, again, should the downfall of the utter villain be exhibited. A plot of this kind would, doubtless, satisfy the moral sense, but it would inspire neither pity nor fear; for pity is aroused by unmerited misfortune, fear by the misfortune of a man like ourselves. Such an event, therefore, will be neither pitiful nor terrible. There remains, then, the charac- 3 ter between these two extremes—that of a man who is not eminently good and just, yet whose misfortune is brought about not by vice or depravity, but by some error or frailty. He must be one who is highly renowned and prosperous—a personage like Oedipus, Thyestes, or other illustrious men of such families.

A well-constructed plot should, therefore, be 4 single in its issue, rather than double as some maintain. The change of fortune should be not from bad to good, but, reversely, from good to bad. It should come about as the result not of vice, but of some great error or frailty, in a character either such as we have described, or better rather than worse. The 5 practice of the stage bears out our view. At first the poets recounted any legend that came in their way. Now, the best tragedies are founded on the story of a few houses—on the fortunes of Alcmaeon, Oedipus, Orestes, Meleager, Thyestes, Telephus, and those others who have done or suffered something terrible. A tragedy, then, to be perfect according to the rules of art should be of this construction. Hence they are in error who censure 6 Euripides just because he follows this principle in his plays, many of which end unhappily. It is, as we have said, the right ending. The best proof is that, on the stage and in dramatic competition, such plays, if well worked out, are the most tragic in effect; and Euripides, faulty though he may be in the general management of his subject, yet is felt to be the most tragic of the poets.

In the second rank comes the kind of tragedy 7 which some place first. Like the *Odyssey*, it has a double thread of plot, and also an opposite catastrophe for the good and for the bad. It is accounted the best because of the weakness of the spectators; for the poet is guided in what he writes by the wishes of his audience. The pleasure, however, 8 thence derived is not the true tragic pleasure. It is proper rather to Comedy, where those who, in the piece, are the deadliest enemies—like Orestes and Aegisthus—quit the stage as friends at the close, and no one slays or is slain.

# XIV

FEAR AND PITY MAY BE aroused by spectacular means; but they may also result from the inner structure of the piece, which is the better way, and indicates a superior poet. For the plot ought to be so constructed that, even without the aid of the eye, he who hears the tale told will thrill with horror and melt to pity at what takes place. This is the impression we should receive from hearing the story of the *Oedipus*. But to produce 2 this effect by the mere spectacle is a less artistic method, and dependent on extraneous aids. Those who employ spectacular means to create a sense not of the terrible but only the monstrous, are strangers to the purpose of Tragedy; for we must not demand of Tragedy any and every kind of pleasure, but only that which is proper to it. And since the pleasure 3 which the poet should afford is that which comes from pity and fear through imitation, it is evident that this quality must be impressed upon the incidents.

Let us then determine what are the circumstances which strike us as terrible or pitiful.

Actions capable of this effect must happen be- 4 tween persons who are either friends or enemies or indifferent to one another. If an enemy kills an enemy, there is nothing to excite pity either in the act or the intention—except so far as the suffering in itself is pitiful. So again with indifferent persons. But when the tragic incident occurs between those who are near or dear to one another—if, for example, a brother kills, or intends to kill, a brother, a son his father, a mother her son, a son his mother, or any other deed of the kind is done—these are the situations to be looked for by the poet. He may not indeed destroy the framework of the received legends—the fact for instance, that Clytemnestra 5 was slain by Orestes and Eriphyle by Alcmaeon— but he ought to show invention of his own, and skillfully handle the traditional material. Let us explain more clearly what is meant by skillful handling.

The action may be done consciously and with 6 knowledge of the persons, in the manner of the older poets. It is thus too that Euripides makes Medea slay her children. Or, again, the deed of horror may be done, but done in ignorance, and the tie of kinship or friendship be discovered afterwards. The *Oedipus* of Sophocles is an example. Here, indeed, the incident is outside the drama proper; but cases occur where it falls within the action of the play: one may cite the *Alcmaeon* of Astydamas, or Telegonus in the *Wounded Odysseus*. Again, there is a third case—<to be about to act 7 with knowledge of the persons and then not to act. The fourth case is> when someone is about to do

an irreparable deed through ignorance, and makes
the discovery before it is done. These are the only
possible ways. For the deed must either be done or
not done—and that wittingly or unwittingly. But
of all these ways, to be about to act knowing the
persons, and then not to act, is the worst. It is shock-
ing without being tragic, for no disaster follows.
It is, therefore, never, or very rarely, found in
poetry. One instance, however, is in the *Antigone*,
where Haemon threatens to kill Creon. The next 8
and better way is that the deed should be perpetrated. Still better, that it should be perpetrated in
ignorance, and the discovery made afterwards. There
is then nothing to shock us, while the discovery
produces a startling effect. The last case is the best, 9
as when in the *Cresphontes* Merope is about to slay
her son, but, recognizing who he is, spares his life.
So in the *Iphigenia*, the sister recognizes the brother
just in time. Again in the *Helle*, the son recognizes
the mother when on the point of giving her up.
This, then, is why a few families only, as has been
already observed, furnish the subjects of tragedy.
It was not art, but happy chance, that led the poets
in search of subjects to impress the tragic quality
upon their plots. They are compelled, therefore, to
have recourse to those houses whose history contains
moving incidents like these.

Enough has now been said concerning the structure of the incidents, and the right kind of plot.

# XV

IN RESPECT OF CHARACTER
there are four things to be aimed at. First, and most
important, it must be good. Now any speech or
action that manifests moral purpose of any kind will
be expressive of character: the character will be
good if the purpose is good. This rule is relative to
each class. Even a woman may be good, and also a
slave; though the woman may be said to be an inferior being, and the slave quite worthless. The 2
second thing to aim at is propriety. There is a type
of manly valor; but valor in a woman, or unscru-
pulous cleverness, is inappropriate. Thirdly, charac- 3
ter must be true to life: for this is a distinct thing
from goodness and propriety, as here described.
The fourth point is consistency, for though the sub- 4
ject of the imitation, who suggested the type, be
inconsistent, still he must be consistently inconsistent. As an example of motiveless degradation of 5
character we have Menelaus in the *Orestes;* of character indecorous and inappropriate, the lament of

Odysseus in the *Scylla*, and the speech of Melanippe;
of inconsistency, the *Iphigenia at Aulis*—for Iphigenia the suppliant in no way resembles her later self.

As in the structure of the plot, so too in the por-  6
traiture of character, the poet should always aim
either at the necessary or the probable. Thus a person of a given character should speak or act in a
given way, by the rule either of necessity or of
probability, just as this event should follow that by
necessary or probable sequence. It is therefore evi-  7
dent that the unraveling of the plot, no less than
the complication, must arise out of the plot itself,
it must not be brought about by the *Deus ex
Machina*—as in the *Medea*, or in the Return of the
Greeks in the *Iliad*. The *Deus ex Machina* should be
employed only for events external to the drama—
for antecedent or subsequent events, which lie beyond the range of human knowledge, and which
require to be reported or foretold; for to the gods
we ascribe the power of seeing all things. Within
the action there must be nothing irrational. If the
irrational cannot be excluded, it should be outside
the scope of the tragedy. Such is the irrational
element in the *Oedipus* of Sophocles.

Again, since Tragedy is an imitation of persons  8
who are above the common level, the example of
good portrait painters should be followed. They,
while reproducing the distinctive form of the
original, make a likeness which is true to life and
yet more beautiful. So too the poet, in representing
men who are irascible or indolent, or have other
defects of character, should preserve the type and
yet ennoble it. In this way Achilles is portrayed by
Agathon and Homer.

These then are rules the poet should observe. Nor  9

should he neglect those appeals to the senses, which, though not among the essentials, are the concomitants of poetry; for here too there is much room for error. But of this enough has been said in our published treatises.

# XVI

WHAT RECOGNITION IS HAS
been already explained. We will now enumerate its
kinds.

First, the least artistic form, which, from poverty
of wit, is most commonly employed—recognition by
signs. Of these some are congenital—such as "the 2
spear which the earth-born race bear on their
bodies," or the stars introduced by Carcinus in his
*Thyestes*. Others are acquired after birth, and of
these some are bodily marks, as scars; some external
tokens, as necklaces, or the little ark in the *Tyro*
by which the discovery is effected. Even these admit 3
of more or less skillful treatment. Thus in the recognition of Odysseus by his scar, the discovery is made
in one way by the nurse, in another by the swine-
herds. The use of tokens for the express purpose of
proof—and, indeed, any formal proof with or without tokens—is a less artistic mode of recognition. A
better kind is that which comes about by a turn of
incident, as in the Bath Scene in the *Odyssey*.

Next come the recognitions invented at will by 4
the poet, and on that account wanting in art. For
example, Orestes in the *Iphigenia* reveals the fact
that he is Orestes. She, indeed, makes herself known
by the letter; but he, by speaking himself and saying
what the poet, not what the plot, requires. This,
therefore, is nearly allied to the fault above mentioned, for Orestes might as well have brought
tokens with him. Another similar instance is the
"voice of the shuttle" in the *Tereus* of Sophocles.

The third kind depends on memory when the 5
sight of some object awakens a feeling: as in the
*Cyprians* of Dicaeogenes, where the hero breaks into
tears on seeing the picture; or again in the *Lay of
Alcinous*, where Odysseus, hearing the minstrel play
the lyre, recalls the past and weeps, and hence the
recognition.

The fourth kind is by process of reasoning. Thus 6
in the *Choëphori:* "Someone resembling me has
come: no one resembles me but Orestes: therefore
Orestes has come." Such too is the discovery made
by Iphigenia in the play of Polyidus the Sophist. It
was a natural reflection for Orestes to make, "So I
too must die at the altar like my sister." So, again,
in the *Tydeus* of Theodectes, the father says, "I
came to find my son, and I lose my own life." So
too in the *Phineidae:* the women, on seeing the place,
inferred their fate—"Here we are doomed to die,
for here we were cast forth." Again, there is a 7
composite kind of recognition involving false inference on the part of one of the characters, as in
the Odysseus Disguised as a Messenger. A said <that
no one else was able to bend the bow; . . . hence B
(the disguised Odysseus) imagined that A would>
recognize the bow which, in fact, he had not seen;

and to bring about a recognition by this means—
the expectation that A would recognize the bow—
is false inference.

But, of all recognitions, the best is that which 8
arises from the incidents themselves, where the
startling discovery is made by natural means. Such
is that in the *Oedipus* of Sophocles, and in the
*Iphigenia;* for it was natural that Iphigenia should
wish to dispatch a letter. These recognitions alone
dispense with the artificial aid of tokens or amulets.
Next come the recognitions by process of reasoning.

# XVII

In constructing the plot and working it out with the proper diction, the poet should place the scene, as far as possible, before his eyes. In this way, seeing everything with the utmost vividness, as if he were a spectator of the action, he will discover what is in keeping with it, and be most unlikely to overlook inconsistencies. The need of such a rule is shown by the fault found in Carcinus. Amphiaraus was on his way from the temple. This fact escaped the observation of one who did not see the situation. On the stage, however, the piece failed, the audience being offended at the oversight.

Again, the poet should work out his play, to the 2 best of his power, with appropriate gestures; for those who feel emotion are most convincing through natural sympathy with the characters they represent; and one who is agitated storms, one who is angry rages, with the most lifelike reality. Hence poetry implies either a happy gift of nature or a strain of madness. In the one case a man can take the mold of any character; in the other, he is lifted out of his proper self.

As for the story, whether the poet takes it ready 3 made or constructs it for himself, he should first sketch its general outline, and then fill in the episodes and amplify in detail. The general plan may be illustrated by the *Iphigenia*. A young girl is sacrificed; she disappears mysteriously from the eyes of those who sacrificed her; she is transported to another country, where the custom is to offer up all strangers to the goddess. To this ministry she is appointed. Sometime later her own brother chances to arrive. The fact that the oracle for some reason ordered him to go there, is outside the general plan of the play. The purpose, again, of his coming is outside the action proper. However, he comes, he is seized, and, when on the point of being sacrificed, reveals who he is. The mode of recognition may be either that of Euripides or of Polyidus, in whose play he exclaims very naturally: "So it was not my sister only, but I too, who was doomed to be sacrificed"; and by that remark he is saved.

After this, the names being once given, it remains 4 to fill in the episodes. We must see that they are relevant to the action. In the case of Orestes, for example, there is the madness which led to his capture, and his deliverance by means of the purificatory rite. In the drama, the episodes are short, 5 but it is these that give extension to Epic poetry. Thus the story of the *Odyssey* can be stated briefly. A certain man is absent from home for many years; he is jealously watched by Poseidon, and left desolate. Meanwhile his home is in a wretched plight —suitors are wasting his substance and plotting

against his son. At length, tempest-tossed, he himself arrives; he makes certain persons acquainted
with him; he attacks the suitors with his own hand,
and is himself preserved while he destroys them.
This is the essence of the plot; the rest is episode.

# XVIII

EVERY TRAGEDY FALLS INTO
two parts—Complication and Unraveling or Denouement. Incidents extraneous to the action are
frequently combined with a portion of the action
proper, to form the Complication; the rest is the
Unraveling. By the Complication I mean all that
extends from the beginning of the action to the part
which marks the turning point to good or bad
fortune. The Unraveling is that which extends from
the beginning of the change to the end. Thus, in
the *Lynceus* of Theodectes the Complication consists of the incidents presupposed in the drama, the
seizure of the child, and then again * * <The
Unraveling> extends from the accusation of murder
to the end.

There are four kinds of Tragedy: the Complex, 2
depending entirely on Reversal of the Situation and
Recognition; the Pathetic (where the motive is
passion)—such as the tragedies on Ajax and Ixion;
the Ethical (where the motives are ethical)—such

as the *Phthiotides* and the *Peleus.* The fourth kind
is the Simple. <We here exclude the purely spectacular element>, exemplified by the *Phorcides,* the
*Prometheus,* and scenes laid in Hades. The poet 3
should endeavor, if possible, to combine all poetic
elements; or, failing that, the greatest number and
those the most important; the more so, in face of
the caviling criticism of the day. For whereas there
have hitherto been good poets, each in his own
branch, the critics now expect one man to surpass
all others in their several lines of excellence.

In speaking of a tragedy as the same or different,
the best test to take is the plot. Identity exists where
the Complication and Unraveling are the same.
Many poets tie the knot well, but unravel it ill. Both
arts, however, should always be mastered.

Again, the poet should remember what has been 4
often said, and not make an Epic structure into a
Tragedy—by an Epic structure I mean one with a
multiplicity of plots—as if, for instance, you were
to make a tragedy out of the entire story of the
*Iliad.* In the Epic poem, owing to its length, each
part assumes its proper magnitude. In the drama the
result is far from answering to the poet's expectation. The proof is that the poets who have drama- 5
tized the whole story of the Fall of Troy, instead of
selecting portions, like Euripides, or who have taken
the whole tale of Niobe, and not a part of her story,
like Aeschylus, either fail utterly or meet with poor
success on the stage. Even Agathon has been known
to fail from this one defect. In his Reversals of the
Situation, however, he shows a marvelous skill in
the effort to hit the popular taste—to produce a
tragic effect that satisfies the moral sense. This effect 6
is produced when the clever rogue, like Sisyphus, is

outwitted, or the brave villain defeated. Such an event is probable in Agathon's sense of the word: "it is probable," he says, "that many things should happen contrary to probability."

The Chorus too should be regarded as one of the 7 actors; it should be an integral part of the whole, and share in the action, in the manner not of Euripides but of Sophocles. As for the later poets, their choral songs pertain as little to the subject of the piece as to that of any other tragedy. They are, therefore, sung as mere interludes—a practice first begun by Agathon. Yet what difference is there between introducing such choral interludes and transferring a speech, or even a whole act, from one play to another?

# XIX

IT REMAINS TO SPEAK OF Diction and Thought, the other parts of Tragedy having been already discussed. Concerning Thought, we may assume what is said in the Rhetoric, to which inquiry the subject more strictly belongs. Under Thought is included every effect which has 2 to be produced by speech, the subdivisions being— proof and refutation; the excitation of the feelings, such as pity, fear, anger, and the like; the suggestion of importance or its opposite. Now, it is evident 3 that the dramatic incidents must be treated from the same points of view as the dramatic speeches, when the object is to evoke the sense of pity, fear, importance, or probability. The only difference is that the incidents should speak for themselves without verbal exposition; while the effects aimed at in speech should be produced by the speaker, and as a result of the speech. For what were the business of a speaker, if the Thought were revealed quite apart from what he says?

Next, as regards Diction. One branch of the in- 4
quiry treats of the Modes of Utterance. But this
province of knowledge belongs to the art of Delivery and to the masters of that science. It includes,
for instance—what is a command, a prayer, a statement, a threat, a question, an answer, and so forth.
To know or not to know these things involves no 5
serious censure upon the poet's art. For who can
admit the fault imputed to Homer by Protagoras—
that in the words, "Sing, goddess, of the wrath," he
gives a command under the idea that he utters a
prayer? For to tell someone to do a thing or not to
do it is, he says, a command. We may, therefore,
pass this over as an inquiry that belongs to another
art, not to poetry.

# XX

[LANGUAGE IN GENERAL in-
cludes the following parts: Letter, Syllable, Connecting word, Noun, Verb, Inflection or Case,
Sentence or Phrase.

A Letter is an indivisible sound, yet not every 2
such sound, but only one which can form part of a
group of sounds. For even brutes utter indivisible
sounds, none of which I call a letter. The sound I 3
mean may be either a vowel, a semivowel, or a mute.
A vowel is that which without impact of tongue or
lip has an audible sound. A semivowel, that which
with such impact has an audible sound, as S and R.
A mute, that which with such impact has by itself
no sound, but joined to a vowel sound becomes
audible, as G and D. These are distinguished ac- 4
cording to the form assumed by the mouth and the
place where they are produced; according as they
are aspirated or smooth, long or short; as they are
acute, grave, or of an intermediate tone; which inquiry belongs in detail to the writers on meter.

A Syllable is a nonsignificant sound, composed of 5 a mute and a vowel: for GR without A is a syllable, as also with A—GRA. But the investigation of these differences belongs also to metrical science.

A Connecting word is a nonsignificant sound 6 which neither causes nor hinders the union of many sounds into one significant sound; it may be placed at either end or in the middle of a sentence. Or, a nonsignificant sound which out of several sounds, each of them significant, is capable of forming one significant sound—as ἀμφί, περί, and the like. Or, 7 a nonsignificant sound which marks the beginning, end, or division of a sentence; such, however, that it cannot correctly stand by itself at the beginning of a sentence—as μέν, ἤτοι, δέ.

A noun is a composite significant sound, not 8 marking time, of which no part is in itself significant: for in double or compound words we do not employ the separate parts as if each were in itself significant. Thus in Theodorus, "god-given," the δῶρον or "gift" is not in itself significant.

A Verb is a composite significant sound, marking 9 time, in which, as in the noun, no part is in itself significant. For "man," or "white" does not express the idea of "when"; but "he walks," or "he has walked" does connote time, present or past.

Inflection belongs both to the noun and verb, and 10 expresses either the relation "of," "to," or the like; or that of number, whether one or many, as "man" or "men"; or the modes or tones in actual delivery, e.g., a question or a command. "Did he go?" and "go" are verbal inflections of this kind.

A Sentence or Phrase is a composite significant 11 sound, some at least of whose parts are in themselves significant; for not every such group of words consists of verbs and nouns—"the definition of man," for example—but it may dispense even with the verb. Still it will always have some significant part, as "in walking," or "Cleon son of Cleon." A sen- 12 tence or phrase may form a unity in two ways— either as signifying one thing, or as consisting of several parts linked together. Thus the *Iliad* is one by the linking together of parts, the definition of man by the unity of the thing signified.]

# XXI

WORDS ARE OF TWO KINDS,
simple and double. By simple I mean those composed of nonsignificant elements, such as γῆ. By double or compound, those composed either of a significant and nonsignificant element (though within the whole word no element is significant), or of elements that are both significant. A word may likewise be triple, quadruple, or multiple in form, like so many Massilian expressions, e.g., "Hermo-caico-xanthus <who prayed to Father Zeus>."

Every word is either current, or strange, or [2] metaphorical, or ornamental, or newly coined, or lengthened, or contracted, or altered.

By a current or proper word I mean one which is [3] in general use among a people; by a strange word, one which is in use in another country. Plainly, therefore, the same word may be at once strange and current, but not in relation to the same people.

The word σίγυνον, "lance," is to the Cyprians a current term but to us a strange one.

Metaphor is the application of an alien name by 4 transference either from genus to species, or from species to genus, or from species to species, or by analogy, that is, proportion. Thus from genus to 5 species, as: "There lies my ship"; for lying at anchor is a species of lying. From species to genus, as: "Verily ten thousand noble deeds hath Odysseus wrought"; for ten thousand is a species of large number, and is here used for a large number generally. From species to species, as: "With blade of bronze drew away the life," and "Cleft the water with the vessel of unyielding bronze." Here ἀρύσαι, "to draw away," is used for ταμεῖν, "to cleave," and ταμεῖν again for ἀρύσαι—each being a species of taking away. Analogy or proportion is when the 6 second term is to the first as the fourth to the third. We may then use the fourth for the second, or the second for the fourth. Sometimes too we qualify the metaphor by adding the term to which the proper word is relative. Thus the cup is to Dionysus as the shield to Ares. The cup may, therefore, be called "the shield of Dionysus," and the shield "the cup of Ares." Or, again, as old age is to life, so is evening to day. Evening may therefore be called "the old age of the day," and old age, "the evening of life," or, in the phrase of Empedocles, "life's setting sun." For some of the terms of the 7 proportion there is at times no word in existence; still the metaphor may be used. For instance, to scatter seed is called sowing: but the action of the sun in scattering his rays is nameless. Still this process bears to the sun the same relation as sowing to the seed. Hence the expression of the poet

"sowing the god-created light." There is another 8
way in which this kind of metaphor may be employed. We may apply an alien term, and then
deny of that term one of its proper attributes; as
if we were to call the shield, not "the cup of Ares,"
but "the wineless cup."

<An ornamental word . . .>

A newly coined word is one which has never 9
been even in local use, but is adopted by the poet
himself. Some such words there appear to be: as
ἐρνύγες, "sprouters," for κέρατα, "horns," and ἀρητήρ,
"supplicator," for ἱερεύς, "priest."

A word is lengthened when its own vowel is 10
exchanged for a longer one, or when a syllable is
inserted. A word is contracted when some part of
it is removed. Instances of lengthening are—πόληος
for πόλεως, and Πηληιάδεω for Πηλείδου; of contraction—κρῖ, δῶ, and ὄψ, as in μία γίνεται ἀμφοτέρων ὄψ.

An altered word is one in which part of the 11
ordinary form is left unchanged, and part is recast;
as, in δεξιτερὸν κατὰ μαζόν, δεξιτερόν is for δεξιόν.

[Nouns in themselves are either masculine, 12
feminine, or neuter. Masculine are such as end in
ν, ρ, ς, or in some letter compounded with ς—these
being two, ψ and ξ. Feminine, such as end in vowels
that are always long, namely η and ω, and—of
vowels that admit of lengthening—those in α. Thus
the number of letters in which nouns masculine and
feminine end is the same; for ψ and ξ are equivalent
to endings in ς. No noun ends in a mute or a vowel
short by nature. Three only end in ι,—μέλι, κόμμι,
πέπερι: five end in υ. Neuter nouns end in these two
latter vowels; also in ν and ς.]

# XXII

THE PERFECTION OF STYLE IS
to be clear without being mean. The clearest style
is that which uses only current or proper words;
at the same time it is mean—witness the poetry of
Cleophon and of Sthenelus. That diction, on the
other hand, is lofty and raised above the commonplace which employs unusual words. By unusual,
I mean strange (or rare) words, metaphorical,
lengthened—anything, in short, that differs from
the normal idiom. Yet a style wholly composed of 2
such words is either a riddle or a jargon; a riddle,
if it consists of metaphors; a jargon, if it consists of
strange (or rare) words. For the essence of a riddle
is to express true facts under impossible combina-
tions. Now this cannot be done by any arrangement
of ordinary words, but by the use of metaphor it
can. Such is the riddle: "A man I saw who on
another man had glued the bronze by aid of fire,"
and others of the same kind. A diction that is made
up of strange (or rare) terms is a jargon. A certain 3

infusion, therefore, of these elements is necessary to style; for the strange (or rare) word, the metaphorical, the ornamental, and the other kinds above mentioned, will raise it above the commonplace and mean, while the use of proper words will make it perspicuous. But nothing contributes more to pro- 4 duce a clearness of diction that is remote from commonness than the lengthening, contraction, and alteration of words. For by deviating in exceptional cases from the normal idiom, the language will gain distinction; while, at the same time, the partial conformity with usage will give perspicuity. The 5 critics, therefore, are in error who censure these licenses of speech, and hold the author up to ridicule. Thus Eucleides the elder declared that it would be an easy matter to be a poet if you might lengthen syllables at will. He caricatured the practice in the very form of his diction, as in the verse:

'Επιχάρην εἶδον Μαραθῶνάδε βαδίζοντα,

or,

οὐκ ἄν γ' ἐράμενος τὸν ἐκείνου ἐλλέβορον.

To employ such license at all obtrusively is, no 6 doubt, grotesque; but in any mode of poetic diction there must be moderation. Even metaphors, strange (or rare) words, or any similar forms of speech, would produce the like effect if used without propriety and with the express purpose of being ludicrous. How great a difference is made by the 7 appropriate use of lengthening, may be seen in Epic poetry by the insertion of ordinary forms in the verse. So, again, if we take a strange (or rare) word, a metaphor, or any similar mode of expres-

sion, and replace it by the current or proper term,
the truth of our observation will be manifest. For
example, Aeschylus and Euripides each composed
the same iambic line. But the alteration of a single
word by Euripides, who employed the rarer term
instead of the ordinary one, makes one verse appear
beautiful and the other trivial. Aeschylus in his
*Philoctetes* says:

$$\phi\alpha\gamma\epsilon\delta\alpha\iota\nu\alpha <\delta'> \,\, \mathring{\eta} \,\, \mu o\upsilon \,\, \sigma\acute{\alpha}\rho\kappa\alpha\varsigma \,\, \mathring{\epsilon}\sigma\theta\acute{\iota}\epsilon\iota \,\, \pi o\delta\acute{o}\varsigma\cdot$$

Euripides substitutes θοινᾶται "feasts on" for ἐσθίει
"feeds on." Again, in the line,

$$\nu\mathring{v}\nu \,\, \delta\acute{\epsilon} \,\, \mu' \,\, \mathring{\epsilon}\mathring{\omega}\nu \,\, \mathring{o}\lambda\acute{\iota}\gamma o\varsigma \,\, \tau\epsilon \,\, \kappa\alpha\mathring{\iota} \,\, o\mathring{v}\tau\iota\delta\alpha\nu\mathring{o}\varsigma \,\, \kappa\alpha\mathring{\iota} \,\, \mathring{\alpha}\epsilon\iota\kappa\acute{\eta}\varsigma,$$

the difference will be felt if we substitute the
common words,

$$\nu\mathring{v}\nu \,\, \delta\acute{\epsilon} \,\, \mu' \,\, \mathring{\epsilon}\mathring{\omega}\nu \,\, \mu\iota\kappa\rho\acute{o}\varsigma \,\, \tau\epsilon \,\, \kappa\alpha\mathring{\iota} \,\, \mathring{\alpha}\sigma\theta\epsilon\nu\iota\kappa\grave{o}\varsigma \,\, \kappa\alpha\mathring{\iota} \,\, \mathring{\alpha}\epsilon\iota\delta\acute{\eta}\varsigma.$$

Or if for the line,

$$\delta\acute{\iota}\phi\rho o\nu \,\, \mathring{\alpha}\epsilon\iota\kappa\acute{\epsilon}\lambda\iota o\nu \,\, \kappa\alpha\tau\alpha\theta\epsilon\mathring{\iota}\varsigma \,\, \mathring{o}\lambda\acute{\iota}\gamma\eta\nu \,\, \tau\epsilon \,\, \tau\rho\acute{\alpha}\pi\epsilon\zeta\alpha\nu,$$

we read,

$$\delta\acute{\iota}\phi\rho o\nu \,\, \mu o\chi\theta\eta\rho\grave{o}\nu \,\, \kappa\alpha\tau\alpha\theta\epsilon\mathring{\iota}\varsigma \,\, \mu\iota\kappa\rho\acute{\alpha}\nu \,\, \tau\epsilon \,\, \tau\rho\acute{\alpha}\pi\epsilon\zeta\alpha\nu.$$

Or for ἠιόνες βοόωσιν, ἠιόνες κράζουσιν.

Again, Ariphrades ridiculed the tragedians for 8
using phrases which no one would employ in
ordinary speech: for example, δωμάτων ἄπο instead of
ἀπὸ δωμάτων, σέθεν, ἐγὼ δέ νιν, Ἀχιλλέως πέρι instead
of περὶ Ἀχιλλέως, and the like. It is precisely because such phrases are not part of the current idiom
that they give distinction to the style. This, however, he failed to see.

It is a great matter to observe propriety in these 9
several modes of expression, as also in compound

words, strange (or rare) words, and so forth. But
the greatest thing by far is to have a command of
metaphor. This alone cannot be imparted by
another; it is the mark of genius, for to make
good metaphors implies an eye for resemblances.

Of the various kinds of words, the compound are 10
best adapted to dithyrambs, rare words to heroic
poetry, metaphors to iambic. In heroic poetry,
indeed, all these varieties are serviceable. But in
iambic verse, which reproduces, as far as may be,
familiar speech, the most appropriate words are
those which are found even in prose. These are—
the current or proper, the metaphorical, the ornamental.

Concerning Tragedy and imitation by means of
action this may suffice.

# XXIII

AS TO THAT POETIC IMITATION which is narrative in form and employs a single meter, the plot manifestly ought, as in a tragedy, to be constructed on dramatic principles. It should have for its subject a single action, whole and complete, with a beginning, a middle, and an end. It will thus resemble a living organism in all its unity, and produce the pleasure proper to it. It will differ in structure from historical compositions, which of necessity present, not a single action, but a single period, and all that happened within that period to one person or to many, little connected together as the events may be. For as the sea fight at Salamis 2 and the battle with the Carthaginians in Sicily took place at the same time, but did not tend to any one result, so in the sequence of events one thing sometimes follows another, and yet no single result is thereby produced. Such is the practice, we may say, of most poets. Here again, then, as has been already 3 observed, the transcendent excellence of Homer is manifest. He never attempts to make the whole war of Troy the subject of his poem, though that war had a beginning and an end. It would have been too vast a theme, and not easily embraced in a single view. If, again, he had kept it within moderate limits, it must have been overcomplicated by the variety of the incidents. As it is, he detaches a single portion, and admits as episodes many events from the general story of the war—such as the Catalogue of the ships and others—thus diversifying the poem. All other poets take a single hero, a single period, or an action single, indeed, but with a multiplicity of parts. Thus did the author of the *Cypria* and of the *Little Iliad*. For this reason the *Iliad* and the *Odyssey* each fur- 4 nish the subject of one tragedy, or, at most, of two; while the *Cypria* supplies materials for many, and the *Little Iliad* for eight—the Award of the Arms, the Philoctetes, the Neoptolemus, the Eurypylus, the Mendicant Odysseus, the Laconian Women, the Fall of Ilium, the Departure of the Fleet.

# XXIV

AGAIN, EPIC POETRY MUST
have as many kinds as Tragedy: it must be simple,
or complex, or "ethical," or "pathetic." The parts
also, with the exception of Song and Spectacle, are
the same; for it requires Reversals of the Situation,
Recognitions, and Scenes of Suffering. Moreover, 2
the thoughts and the diction must be artistic. In all
these respects Homer is our earliest and sufficient
model. Indeed, each of his poems has a twofold
character. The *Iliad* is at once simple and "pathetic," and the *Odyssey* complex (for Recognition
scenes run through it), and at the same time "ethical." Moreover, in diction and thought they are
supreme.

Epic poetry differs from Tragedy in the scale on 3
which it is constructed, and in its meter. As regards
scale or length, we have already laid down an adequate limit: the beginning and the end must be capable of being brought within a single view. This
condition will be satisfied by poems on a smaller

scale than the old epics, and answering in length
to the group of tragedies presented at a single sit-
ting.

Epic poetry has, however, a great—a special— 4
capacity for enlarging its dimensions, and we can
see the reason. In Tragedy we cannot imitate several lines of actions carried on at one and the same
time; we must confine ourselves to the action on
the stage and the part taken by the players. But in
Epic poetry, owing to the narrative form, many
events simultaneously transacted can be presented;
and these, if relevant to the subject, add mass and
dignity to the poem. The Epic has here an advan-
tage, and one that conduces to grandeur of effect,
to diverting the mind of the hearer, and relieving
the story with varying episodes. For sameness of
incident soon produces satiety, and makes tragedies fail on the stage.

As for the meter, the heroic measure has proved 5
its fitness by the test of experience. If a narrative
poem in any other meter or in many meters were
now composed, it would be found incongruous. For
of all measures the heroic is the stateliest and the
most massive; and hence it most readily admits rare
words and metaphors, which is another point in
which the narrative form of imitation stands alone.
On the other hand, the iambic and the trochaic
tetrameter are stirring measures, the latter being
akin to dancing, the former expressive of action.
Still more absurd would it be to mix together dif- 6
ferent meters, as was done by Chaeremon. Hence
no one has ever composed a poem on a great scale
in any other than heroic verse. Nature herself, as
we have said, teaches the choice of the proper measure.

Homer, admirable in all respects, has the special 7
merit of being the only poet who rightly appre-
ciates the part he should take himself. The poet
should speak as little as possible in his own person,
for it is not this that makes him an imitator. Other
poets appear themselves upon the scene throughout,
and imitate but little and rarely. Homer, after a few
prefatory words, at once brings in a man, or
woman, or other personage, none of them wanting
in characteristic qualities, but each with a character of his own.

The element of the wonderful is required in 8
Tragedy. The irrational, on which the wonderful
depends for its chief effects, has wider scope in
Epic poetry, because there the person acting is not
seen. Thus, the pursuit of Hector would be ludicrous if placed upon the stage—the Greeks stand-
ing still and not joining in the pursuit, and Achilles
waving them back. But in the Epic poem the absurdity passes unnoticed. Now the wonderful is
pleasing, as may be inferred from the fact that
everyone tells a story with some addition of his
own, knowing that his hearers like it. It is Homer 9
who has chiefly taught other poets the art of telling
lies skillfully. The secret of it lies in a fallacy. For,
assuming that if one thing is or becomes, a second
is or becomes, men imagine that, if the second is, the
first likewise is or becomes. But this is a false inference. Hence, where the first thing is untrue, it
is quite unnecessary, provided the second be true,
to add that the first is or has become. For the mind,
knowing the second to be true, falsely infers the
truth of the first. There is an example of this in
the Bath Scene of the *Odyssey*.

Accordingly, the poet should prefer probable 10

impossibilities to improbable possibilities. The tragic
plot must not be composed of irrational parts.
Everything irrational should, if possible, be excluded; or, at all events, it should lie outside the
action of the play (as, in the *Oedipus*, the hero's
ignorance as to the manner of Laius' death); not
within the drama—as, in the *Electra*, the messenger's account of the Pythian games; or, as in the
*Mysians*, the man who has come from Tegea to
Mysia and is still speechless. The plea that otherwise
the plot would have been ruined is ridiculous; such
a plot should not in the first instance be constructed.
But once the irrational has been introduced and an
air of likelihood imparted to it, we must accept it
in spite of the absurdity. Take even the irrational
incidents in the *Odyssey*, where Odysseus is left
upon the shore of Ithaca. How intolerable even
these might have been would be apparent if an inferior poet were to treat the subject. As it is, the
absurdity is veiled by the poetic charm with which
the poet invests it.

The diction should be elaborated in the pauses of 11
the action, where there is no expression of character or thought. For, conversely, character and
thought are merely obscured by a diction that is
overbrilliant.

# XXV

With respect to critical difficulties and their solutions, the number and nature of the sources from which they may be drawn may be thus exhibited.

The poet being an imitator, like a painter or any other artist, must of necessity imitate one of three objects—things as they were or are, things as they are said or thought to be, or things as they ought to be. The vehicle of expression is language—either 2 current terms or, it may be, rare words or metaphors. There are also many modifications of language which we concede to the poets. Add to this 3 that the standard of correctness is not the same in poetry and politics, any more than in poetry and any other art. Within the art of poetry itself there are two kinds of faults—those which touch its essence, and those which are accidental. If a poet has 4 chosen to imitate something, <but has imitated it incorrectly> through want of capacity, the error is inherent in the poetry. But if the failure is due

111

to a wrong choice—if he has represented a horse as throwing out both his off legs at once, or introduced technical inaccuracies in medicine, for example, or in any other art—the error is not essential to the poetry. These are the points of view from which we should consider and answer the objections raised by the critics.

First as to matters which concern the poet's own 5 art. If he describes the impossible, he is guilty of an error; but the error may be justified, if the end of the art be thereby attained (the end being that already mentioned)—if, that is, the effect of this or any other part of the poem is thus rendered more striking. A case in point is the pursuit of Hector. If, however, the end might have been as well, or better, attained without violating the special rules of the poetic art, the error is not justified, for every kind of error should, if possible, be avoided.

Again, does the error touch the essentials of the poetic art, or some accident of it? For example, not to know that a hind has no horns is a less serious matter than to paint it inartistically.

Further, if it be objected that the description is 6 not true to fact, the poet may perhaps reply—"But the objects are as they ought to be": just as Sophocles said that he drew men as they ought to be; Euripides, as they are. In this way the objection may 7 be met. If, however, the representation be of neither kind, the poet may answer—"This is how men say the thing is." This applies to tales about the gods. It may well be that these stories are not higher than fact nor yet true to fact: they are, very possibly, what Xenophanes says of them. But anyhow, "this is what is said." Again, a description may be no better than the fact: still, it was the fact; as in the passage about the arms: "Upright upon their butt-ends stood the spears." This was the custom then, as it now is among the Illyrians.

Again, in examining whether what has been said 8 or done by someone is poetically right or not, we must not look merely to the particular act or saying, and ask whether it is poetically good or bad. We must also consider by whom it is said or done, to whom, when, by what means, or for what end; whether, for instance, it be to secure a greater good, or avert a greater evil.

Other difficulties may be resolved by due regard 9 to the usage of language. We may note a rare word, as in οὐρῆας μὲν πρῶτον, where the poet perhaps employs οὐρῆας not in the sense of mules, but of sentinels. So, again, of Dolon: "ill-favored indeed he was to look upon." It is not meant that his body was ill-shaped, but that his face was ugly; for the Cretans use the word εὐειδές, "well-favored," to denote a fair face. Again, ζωρότερον δὲ κέραιε, "mix the drink livelier," does not mean "mix it stronger" as for hard drinkers, but "mix it quicker."

Sometimes an expression is metaphorical, as "Now 10 all gods and men were sleeping through the night" —while at the same time the poet says: "Often indeed as he turned his gaze to the Trojan plain, he marveled at the sound of flutes and pipes." "All" is here used metaphorically for "many," all being a species of many. So, in the verse "alone she hath no part . . . ," οἴη, "alone," is metaphorical; for the best known may be called the only one.

Again, the solution may depend upon accent or 11 breathing. Thus Hippias of Thasos solved the difficulties in the lines δίδομεν (διδόμεν) δέ οἱ, and τὸ μὲν οὗ (οὐ) καταπύθεται ὄμβρῳ.

Or, again, the question may be solved by punc- 12
tuation, as in Empedocles—"Of a sudden things became mortal that before had learned to be immortal,
and things unmixed before mixed."

Or, again, by ambiguity of meaning—as παρῴ- 13
χηκεν δὲ πλέω νύξ, where the word πλέω is am-
biguous.

Or by the usage of language. Thus any mixed 14
drink is called οἶνος, "wine." Hence Ganymede is
said "to pour the wine to Zeus," though the gods do
not drink wine. So too workers in iron are called
χαλκέας, or workers in bronze. This, however, may
also be taken as a metaphor.

Again, when a word seems to involve some incon- 15
sistency of meaning, we should consider how many
senses it may bear in the particular passage. For 16
example: "there was stayed the spear of bronze"—
we should ask in how many ways we may take
"being checked there." The true mode of interpretation is the precise opposite of what Glaucon men-
tions. Critics, he says, jump at certain groundless
conclusions; they pass adverse judgment and then
proceed to reason on it; and, assuming that the poet
has said whatever they happen to think, find fault
if a thing is inconsistent with their own fancy. The
question about Icarius has been treated in this fash-
ion. The critics imagine he was a Lacedaemonian.
They think it strange, therefore, that Telemachus
should not have met him when he went to Lace-
daemon. But the Cephallenian story may perhaps
be the true one. They allege that Odysseus took a
wife from among themselves, and that her father
was Icadius, not Icarius. It is merely a mistake,
then, that gives plausibility to the objection.

In general, the impossible must be justified by ref- 17

erence to artistic requirements, or to the higher reality, or to received opinion. With respect to the requirements of art, a probable impossibility is to be preferred to a thing improbable and yet possible. Again, it may be impossible that there should be men such as Zeuxis painted. "Yes," we say, "but the impossible is the higher thing; for the ideal type must surpass the reality." To justify the irrational, we appeal to what is commonly said to be. In addition to which, we urge that the irrational sometimes does not violate reason; just as "it is probable that a thing may happen contrary to probability."

Things that sound contradictory should be ex-18 amined by the same rules as in dialectical refutation —whether the same thing is meant, in the same relation, and in the same sense. We should therefore solve the question by reference to what the poet says himself, or to what is tacitly assumed by a person of intelligence.

The element of the irrational, and, similarly, de-19 pravity of character, are justly censured when there is no inner necessity for introducing them. Such is the irrational element in the introduction of Aegeus by Euripides and the badness of Menelaus in the *Orestes*.

Thus, there are five sources from which critical 20 objections are drawn. Things are censured either as impossible, or irrational, or morally hurtful, or contradictory, or contrary to artistic correctness. The answers should be sought under the twelve heads above mentioned.

# XXVI

THE QUESTION MAY BE RAISED
whether the Epic or Tragic mode of imitation is
the higher. If the more refined art is the higher, and
the more refined in every case is that which appeals
to the better sort of audience, the art which imitates anything and everything is manifestly most
unrefined. The audience is supposed to be too dull
to comprehend unless something of their own is
thrown in by the performers, who therefore indulge
in restless movements. Bad flute-players twist and
twirl if they have to represent "the quoit-throw,"
or hustle the coryphaeus when they perform the
*Scylla.* Tragedy, it is said, has this same defect. We 2
may compare the opinion that the older actors en-
tertained of their successors. Mynniscus used to call
Callippides "ape" on account of the extravagance
of his action, and the same view was held of Pin-
darus. Tragic art, then, as a whole, stands to Epic
in the same relation as the younger to the elder
actors. So we are told that Epic poetry is addressed

to a cultivated audience, who do not need gesture; Tragedy, to an inferior public. Being then unre- 3 fined, it is evidently the lower of the two.

Now, in the first place, this censure attaches not to the poetic but to the histrionic art; for gesticulation may be equally overdone in epic recitation, as by Sosistratus, or in lyrical competition, as by Mnasitheus the Opuntian. Next, all action is not to be condemned—any more than all dancing—but only that of bad performers. Such was the fault found in Callippides, as also in others of our own day, who are censured for representing degraded women. Again, Tragedy like Epic poetry produces its effect even without action; it reveals its power by mere reading. If, then, in all other respects it is superior, this fault, we say, is not inherent in it.

And superior it is, because it has all the epic ele- 4 ments—it may even use the epic meter—with the music and spectacular effects as important accessories; and these produce the most vivid of pleasures. Further, it has vividness of impression in reading as well as in representation. Moreover, the art 5 attains its end within narrower limits; for the concentrated effect is more pleasurable than one which is spread over a long time and so diluted. What, for example, would be the effect of the *Oedipus* of Sophocles, if it were cast into a form as long as the *Iliad*? Once more, the Epic imitation has less unity; 6 as is shown by this, that any Epic poem will furnish subjects for several tragedies. Thus if the story adopted by the poet has a strict unity, it must either be concisely told and appear truncated; or, if it conform to the Epic canon of length, it must seem weak and watery. <Such length implies some loss of unity,> if, I mean, the poem is constructed out of several actions, like the *Iliad* and the *Odys-sey*, which have many such parts, each with a certain magnitude of its own. Yet these poems are as perfect as possible in structure; each is, in the highest degree attainable, an imitation of a single action.

If, then, Tragedy is superior to Epic poetry in all 7 these respects, and, moreover, fulfills its specific function better as an art—for each art ought to produce, not any chance pleasure but the pleasure proper to it, as already stated—it plainly follows that Tragedy is the higher art, as attaining its end more perfectly.

Thus much may suffice concerning Tragic and 8 Epic poetry in general; their several kinds and parts, with the number of each and their differences; the causes that make a poem good or bad; the objections of the critics and the answers to these objections. * * *